A day in Pompeii
daily life, culture and society

Eva Cantarella Luciana Jacobelli

A day in Pompeii

daily life, culture and society

electa napoli

Electa Napoli

editing
Silvia Cassani

art director
Enrica D'Aguanno

graphic
Gianni Manna

translation
Jan Gates

Chapters by Eva Cantarella: *Family Life and the Condition of Women, Politics, Religious Life*, and in the section *The City*: Street wolves. *Recreation and Entertainment:* Female prostitution, Male prostitution, Gladiatorial contests. Chapters by Luciana Jacobelli: *The Economy, Housing and Home-life, Roads, Traffic and Public services, Recreation and Entertainment.* The Monuments

Photographs
© for the images: Soprintendenza per i Beni Archeologici di Napoli e Caserta; Soprintendenza Archeologica di Pompei; Archivio dell'Arte-Luciano Pedicini, Napoli. Drawing of the plan of Pompeii by Riccardo Merlo

Contents

Introduction to the history and archaeology of Pompeii

The eruption of Vesuvius

On the 24th August 79 A.D Pompeii perished. On that day Vesuvius suddenly erupted an enormous quantity of lapilli, lava and poisonous gas, which destroyed the city forever, together with its neighbours – Herculaneum, Stabiae and Oplontis.

However unusual it may seem, the event took the Pompeians completely by surprise. They knew that they were living in a seismic region because seventeen years earlier, in 62 AD, a violent earthquake had destroyed or damaged many buildings, several of which had been closed for restoration. In subsequent years, other tremors had probably shaken the region, provoking further damage, which, like that of 62, was still visible at the time of the eruption. In fact, in the year 79 the colonnade of the Basilica was still lying on the ground, only the men's section of the thermal baths in the Forum had been re-opened to the public, of the three public buildings used for performances only the Amphitheatre was accessible, and the Large Palaestra was still under restoration. In short, earthquakes were predictable disasters in Pompeii.

However, nobody was expecting Vesuvius to erupt, given that the last eruption had taken place in the 7th century BC before Pompeii existed. When the long dormant phase of the volcano ended, that 24th August, the explosion was terrifying. This is known both from the results of analysis of deposits of the erupted material and also from an extraordinary, historical document, that is to say two letters written by Pliny the Younger, who described the different phases of the eruption.

Starting with Pliny: when the eruption began he was in Campania with his famous uncle, Pliny the Elder, commander of a fleet based at Misenum. Pliny the Elder lost his life during the eruption, and the historian Tacitus – intending to recount his death – asked Pliny's nephew to describe the events in detail. Pliny the Younger replied with his famous epistle VI, 16.

"It was about one o'clock in the afternoon when my mother drew his (Pliny the Elder's) attention to a cloud of strange size and shape….. My uncle asked for his sandals and went up onto some high ground to observe the phenomenon more easily. From a distant mountain (which he later learnt was Vesuvius), a cloud was rising whose shape was best described as that of a pine tree. Almost resembling a huge trunk, the cloud branched out in height, elevated by an enormous force I believed; and then, gathering strength, or perhaps overcome by its own weight, the cloud spread out, at times snow-white and at others dark and dirty depending on the quantity of ash or earth that it had thrown up."

Like a good naturalist Pliny the Elder decided to put to sea to observe the phenomenon more closely. As his nephew informs us, it was also a noble gesture of friendship: the wife of a friend

Columns of the Forum of Pompeii

*Vesuvius and the
Forum of Pompeii*

who was trapped in her villa in the foothills of Vesuvius had sent a messenger asking for help. The situation was very serious: "The ash already falling on their ships became hotter and denser the closer they got. Blackened stones, burnt and fragmented by the fire, were also falling on them." Pliny disembarked along the Stabian coast while "huge flames and long tongues of fire flickered from different points on Mount Vesuvius, their glares made brighter against the darkness of the night". After having tried to reassure his friends that the flames were only farmers' fires, Pliny, apparently calm, went to sleep. But when he woke up "the courtyard next to the living area (*diaeta*) was already so full of ash and lapilli, that, to remain any longer would

mean certain entrapment." By now there was no chance of escape. The house, almost torn from its foundations, was being shaken backwards and forwards unabatedly by fierce earth tremors, whilst in the open the shower of lapilli, though light, was fearful.

Hoping to protect their heads with pillows, Pliny and his friends came outside where, even though it was morning, a black and gloomy darkness had fallen. At dawn on the 25th August Pliny wanted to reach the beach to try to put to sea, but the sea was still too rough to venture out. The end had come: "...lying on a sheet spread on the ground, Pliny asked twice for water and drank it in one breath.... Supported by two slaves he tried to get up, but fell immediately, because, I believe, his

throat was blocked and his breath suffocated by the ash-filled air. When daylight returned, his body was found intact and uninjured, dressed as before and with all the appearance of a man asleep rather than dead."

After receiving this first letter, Tacitus asked for more information: he wanted to know what was happening at Misenum where Pliny the Younger had remained. Pliny's reply, which describes his adventurous flight to safety, provides additional, important information regarding the catastrophe. (Epistle VI, 20). "The earth had been shaking for many days, but as earthquakes were frequent phenomena in Campania no-one was excessively worried. That night, however, the tremors intensified to such an extent that the world seemed upside down."

When the situation became unbearable, the young Pliny (it was then the morning of the 25th August and his uncle was either dying or dead) decided to leave the city together with his mother: "A dumb-founded crowd followed us… and as we proceeded the huge crowd pursued us …… the carts which we had had brought, even though they were on perfectly flat ground, moved by themselves in different directions and they would not stay still even when boulders were propped against them. As if pushed back by the earth tremors, we saw the sea retreat and the shore widen, leaving the dried up carcasses of many marine creatures on the beach. From the opposite direction, streaked with flashes and blazing steam, a terrifying black cloud frayed into long

*Venus in a chariot,
fresco in the workshop
of Verecundus, Pompeii*

disperse, light returned and the sun reappeared shining but pale as if during an eclipse: "Everything appeared changed and was covered with a thick layer of ash".

An impressive document and at the same time scientifically revealing, Pliny the Younger's description has been used in fact by vulcanologists to try to understand the various phases of the eruption, together with the analysis of the remains of volcanic material. In the first letter the description of the volcanic "pine tree" has been identified with a phase of the eruption termed appropriately "Plinian" by vulcanologists. It is characterised by the emission of a jet of gas and ash thrown up to form a high, magmatic column. This column then falls back to earth in the form of pumice, as described by Pliny and confirmed by the stratigraphic sequence studied at Pompeii. It was found that the size of the pumice stones increased as the eruption proceeded. This means that the energy of the eruption increased with time and that the column was pushed up to ever-greater heights. Since the wind was blowing in a southeasterly direction at that moment, the column fell principally on the eastern and southern slopes of Vesuvius, burying Pompeii. This phase lasted about twelve hours, then the conditions of the eruption changed drastically.

In the second letter Pliny describes other amazing phenomena, which would seem incredible if not confirmed by scientific evidence: the retreat of the sea (*praetera mare in se resorberi*) – which preceded the most disastrous phase of the eruption – and the fall of ash which obscured the daylight. In fact these are typical phenomena of the last phase of this type of eruption. When the eruption seemed to have subsided due to the diminishing pressure of gas, violent jets of steam were produced, fed by water from the fluid rock in the magmatic

streaks of flame, like great bolts of lightening." Taking his mother by the hand and imploring her to hurry, Pliny then tried to escape on foot: "Ash was still falling, though less than before. I turned round. A dense cloud hung behind us". Meanwhile night was falling rapidly: "You could hear the groans of women, the supplicating cries of children, the shouts of men: and those who called out loudly to their parents, children or spouses, and they recognised each others' appeals. There were those who for fear of death prayed to die. Many raised their hands to the gods, while many others cried that there were no longer any gods and that this was the last and eternal night of the world." Finally the mist began to

chamber. The steam, expanding with the speed of a hurricane, destroyed everything it encountered in its path. These were the terrible *surges*, streams of boiling vapour full of ash, which suffocated and killed Pliny the Elder and with him many other Pompeians who tenaciously remained in their homes, or when the eruption seemed to have subsided, returned to collect their most valuable possessions or to rob the houses of the rich. Others were killed by the collapse of their roofs under the weight of the lapilli. It is difficult to estimate the number of dead precisely: probably a thousand out of a population of about ten thousand inhabitants.

The origins and development of Pompeii

When it disappeared in 79 AD Pompeii had a long history behind it. The original nucleus was formed towards the end of the 7th century BC on a rocky spur formed by an ancient lava flow about 25 metres above sea level, and bounded on its western side by the River Sarno. It was a particularly favourable position at the maritime outlet of the rich and productive Campanian, agricultural hinterland and it quickly became a flourishing town. During the first centuries of its existence it underwent the influx of two civilisations which dominated Campania, the Greeks and Etruscans. In fact there has been a long debate between those who maintain that the urban layout of the town can be traced to an "Etruscan Pompeii", and those who emphasise the Hellenistic aspects in its origins. In any case the Etruscans – widely distributed in the area between Capua, Fratte and Pontecagnano – were definitively defeated by a Cuman-Siracusan coalition in 474 BC. Towards the end of the 5th century a new people, the Samnites, came down from their barren mountains and invaded the fertile coastal plains, settling in Pompeii as well as in other places. The influx of the Samnites led to a conspicuous increase in the population and a consequent, urban development in Pompeii. The settlement overtook the dimensions of the ancient nucleus – visible in the southwest – extending north, towards Region VI, and

Plaster cast of the body of a Pompeian attempting to escape from the eruption. Garden of the fugitives, Pompeii

subsequently towards the east. The principal public buildings in Pompeii were built or embellished in this period and there was also a marked expansion in private construction work.

During the final years of Samnite Pompeii the allies of Rome (the *socii italici*), tired of being treated as subjects, took to arms to obtain Roman citizenship. Like other cities in Campania, Pompeii took part in the war and in 89 BC it was besieged by Sulla, who after having conquered it, set up a colony (in 80 B.C) which takes its name from him: *Colonia Cornelia Veneria Pompeianorum*. Cornelio was Sulla's aristocratic name and Venus the goddess to whom he was particularly devoted. Consequently the Romans joined the various ethnic groups already present in the city, and they assumed administrative and political rule. On the whole, the ancient Pompeians and the Romans amalgamated well; the city spread and became more lively and modernised. The principal public buildings and private houses were built or restored according to the styles of the times. The area of greatest expansion continued to be that of the east, around Via dell'Abbondanza, but the southern and western slopes of the city were also areas of major development, which, because of their panoramic position, became the favourite residential areas of the rich. The city had many happy years in which its economy prospered, society became passionately interested in politics, the theatres and amphitheatres held shows and different forms of entertainment and the thermal baths were frequented daily by members of every social class. The first time the peaceful existence of the city was disturbed was in 59 AD when a riot between the Pompeians and Nocerines broke out. The event was serious enough to deserve a mention in the Annals of Tacitus, and resulted in the 'disqualification of the arena' for 10 years. But much more serious was the catastrophic earthquake in 62 AD, which, after two thousand years, has still left traces. At the time of the eruption in 79 much reconstruction work was already under way; in many houses pieces of furniture had been moved from their rooms and stacked in others to allow the fallen and cracked walls to be restored; some of the thermal baths had been closed to the public; the city's water system was partially under restoration and some of the temples had been closed. Recently, however, an hypothesis has been made that not all of the restoration work under way in Pompeii in 79 was due to the earthquake of 62. Probably this was the most important reason and was recorded by historical sources and epigraphs. It is now thought, however, that the catastrophic eruption of 79 AD was preceded by an intensification of seismic activity which caused ulterior damage to those buildings already affected by the earthquake of 62.

The aftermath of the eruption: government aid, private initiative and plunder

After the eruption of Vesuvius, when life returned more or less to normal in the region, Rome sent an investigatory commission composed of two special magistrates the *curatores restituendae Campaniae* (Svet. Titus, VIII, 4; Dio Cass., LXVI, 24, 3-4). Their duty was to save what was salvageable and help the people, but they could do very little: from the ash and lapilli that covered the city only the tops of some columns in the Forum and the highest parts of certain buildings emerged.

In the meantime many private individuals had probably attempted to recover some of their valuables and the usual profiteers had taken advantage of the situation to steal and sell the spoils at high prices. It is likely that a recovery operation was undertaken by central authorities, especially concerning the

The theatre of Herculaneum in a 19th century etching

white and coloured marble, which was systematically stripped from the majority of Pompeii's public buildings.

When the Emperor Titus visited the city in the year 80, he was forced to admit that the *curatores* were right: the city had been destroyed, as confirmed dramatically by literary sources as well: "When the crops have grown again to restore greenery to this desert, will future generations believe that buried cities and populations are lying beneath their feet and that their ancestors' countryside disappeared in a sea of fire?", wrote Statius in 88 AD (*Silv.*, IV, 4, 78-84). And Martialis: "This is Mount Vesuvius, yesterday it was still covered in grass and shaded by vine leaves… now everything lies destroyed by the flames, covered by this sad ash. Not even the gods would have wanted to consent to this" (Mart., IV, 44).

A brief history of the excavations

After the eruption of 79 AD the devastated territory was reoccupied.

Farmers returned to till the earth which in turn began to produce crops. At the beginning of the 3rd century Dio Cassius spoke of the trees and vineyards on Vesuvius (LXVI, 21-22,1). During the 2nd century AD transportation routes were reopened and communications returned to normal. It was only the cities which had disappeared. Even the name of Pompeii was lost; on the site where it had been a small community named Civita was established. It was only in 1592, during the boring of a canal deriving from the River Sarno, that the ruins of certain buildings, inscriptions and coins came to light. But these findings had no follow up, nor did others in subsequent decades.

Finally, a century and a half later, the fortuitous discovery of some works of art in Resina (Herculaneum) received wide acclaim, and led to the start of excavations there (1738). Pompeii was discovered ten years later, and excavations began there too. In 1763 an

Transporting the antiquities of Herculaneum from the Museum of Portici to the Palazzo degli Studi in Naples. An engraving from "Voyage pittoresque ou description des Royaumes de Naples et de Sicile" by the Abbé de Saint-Non, published in Paris in the years 1781-86

On the following page:
Room of a Pompeian lady, by Federico Maldarelli, Provincial Administration, Avellino. In this 19th century painting the artist reproduces objects found in Pompeii, such as the stool in the foreground

inscription was found with mention of the *Respublica Pompeianorum* (CIL X, 1018): Pompeii's identity was finally restored.

The first phase of the excavation was essentially devoted to the recovery of artefacts, rather than bringing the city and its monuments to light. The findings, including many paintings detached from their walls, were transported to the Royal Villa of Portici and subsequently transferred to the Royal Bourbon Museum in Naples, currently the National Archaeological Museum (1805-1822).

After these first sensational findings Europe was flooded by a wave of enthusiasm. Due to the wishes of sovereigns and of their consorts, often enthusiastic scholars of antiquities, the excavations proceeded rapidly between 1770 and 1815. Goethe visited them in 1787. Even the English Ambassador, Sir William Hamilton, took an active interest in the findings in Pompeii, from which he made large profits. Following a series of events, after the Vienna Conference and the return of the Bourbons (1815), Francesco I gave new

impetus to research, and when Garibaldi entered Naples, expelling the Bourbons, the direction of the Royal Museum was entrusted to Alexander Dumas the father (1861). The direction of the excavations was given to Giuseppe Fiorelli (1863-1875), who finally instigated a new phase of research based on scientific rigour. We are indebted to Fiorelli not only for his division of Pompeii into Regions (areas) and *Insulae* (blocks), but also for the method of producing impressive, visible evidence of the agony of the Pompeians, in other words, the casts of the dead bodies left after the eruption. This method consisted in pouring liquid plaster into the cavities left by the decomposition of organic substances in the bank of volcanic ash. Once solidified, the plaster reproduced the exact form of a dead person, animal or plant, with unforgettably dramatic effects.

The society

Family life and the condition of women

Statue of Eumachia, from the building of Eumachia, in Pompeii. National Archaeological Museum, Naples

The family, the power of the father and relationships between generations

In ancient Rome, the group constituted by the name *familia* was very different from the family of today. Not all the members of the *familia* were connected by marriage or by blood, as are the members of a modern family.

The members of the Roman family – wives, children and grandchildren-were all under the legal control (*patria potestas*) of the head of the family. In addition, slaves were members of the *familia* although under different conditions.

To understand the extent of the power of the *paterfamilias* we need to consider what happened to a baby at birth. In Rome and in Roman Pompeii, immediately after the birth, a newborn child was placed at the feet of his father. If the father picked him up (a gesture called *tollere o suscipere liberos*) the newborn child became part of the family. If this did not happen, the child was "*expostus*" (exponere = to place outside), in other words abandoned to his fate. But the power the *paterfamilias* exercised over his children did not cease when a child reached the age of maturity (as under modern law and the laws of other ancient cultures). Instead it lasted for as long as the *pater* was alive, regardless of his children's age. In fact, of all the family, the city recognised only the *paterfamilias* as having full legal capacity in the field of private law, so the entire family estate was his personal property. If one of his

Female portrait, mosaic from Pompeii, house VI, 15, 4. National Archaeological Museum, Naples

Gold bulla *from Pompeii, House of Menander. The* bulla, *a pendant which hung from the neck, identified freeborn children*

descendants acquired possessions, these automatically belonged to the *pater*. If a descendant committed an illegal act the *pater* could free himself of all responsibility by giving the guilty party to the injured party as a slave. In addition, children (both male and female) could not marry without the consent of the father, who, if he changed his mind, could break up their marriages. Finally, whatever the age of the children, they were subject to their father's disciplinary power: he could even inflict severe corporal punishments and, in extreme cases, put them to death.

In the field of public law, however, things were different. Freeborn males, on reaching the age of maturity, acquired legal rights in this field. They had the right to vote in the city's assemblies and could hold public offices, assuming of course that their *pater* was willing to finance this undertaking.

In short, the relationship between the generations was so difficult that some scholars – probably exaggerating, but addressing a real problem – describe a type of national nightmare, in which children desired to kill their father, and fathers were terrified of being killed by their children.

The House of Marcus Lucretius in a 19th century reproduction

Family and slavery

As stated earlier, slaves were part of the family, but considered as objects rather than as human beings, over which the *paterfamilias* exercised a power resembling in many respects that held over his possessions.

There were many ways in which a person might become a slave. The most common and probably the original, was by being captured as a prisoner of war. Another was by being born to a slave Mother. Under Roman law, children born outside marriage followed the condition of their mother from the moment of their birth; a female slave could not marry so her children belonged to her owner. People also became slaves for other reasons, for example, those who avoided doing military service or who avoided the census were sold as slaves.

But what exactly were the conditions of a Roman slave? In early times, when each head of the family provided for his household by the cultivation of his small holding with the help of his children and perhaps a few slaves, there was very little difference between slaves and children (although, obviously, the children became independent on the death of their father whilst the slaves remained in bondage). However, with the passing of time, when the number of slaves increased as a result of Roman conquests and when small holders were replaced by rich landowners, slaves on these large agricultural estates were heavily exploited and often lived on bare subsistence conditions. On the other hand, slaves living in cities, especially when they had some kind of profession (for example as a secretary or tutor) found themselves in highly privileged situations and were even able to save enough money to purchase their freedom.

A freed slave, called "libertus" (in contrast to a man born free, called "ingenuus") was tied to his former owner by a bond of gratitude, which obliged the freedman to perform a series of duties and services, including economic ones (for example, contributing to the dowry of a daughter). But apart from this he was a free man, who might even take over public duties (with some exceptions, for example, the post of decurion, which was reserved exclusively for the "ingenui").

Marriage

Defined by the jurist Modestinus as "a lifetime union", marriage in Rome in reality frequently lasted a short time. In fact, especially during the Imperial age, many marriages ended in divorce, followed, particularly amongst the upper classes, by a second, third or subsequent marriage.

Except in special circumstances, marriage was reserved for Roman citizens of adult age, which started at twelve years old for females and fourteen for males. It was solemnised by a ceremony which began in the morning with the interpretation of omens and sacrifices. A banquet was offered at the bride's house, after which, in the evening, she was accompanied in a torchlight procession to her husband's house (*in domum deductio*), while her husband's friends sang songs extolling his virility. Walnuts were then thrown over the couple to wish them fertility.

Finally, once the bride reached her future home, she crossed the threshold on her husband's arm and offered water and fire to the gods. However, none of these celebrations were indispensable for a marriage settlement: they were only social ceremonies, which, if the marriage was contested, served to distinguish a marriage from concubinage.

In classical times, Roman law required only that a couple, being both Roman citizens and of age should establish and maintain a cohabitation with the intention to be man and wife (*maritalis affectio*). If and when these conditions were no longer met, the marriage was dissolved.

The condition of women

For those wishing to study the condition of women, the city of Pompeii, in its complexity, represents an extraordinary document, capable of illuminating aspects and moments in the lives of women which would otherwise have remained unknown. To understand the importance of the information provided by Pompeii it is necessary to consider, besides the archaeological evidence, what can be reconstructed from written sources, literary and legal. Although they do not make specific reference to Pompeii, these sources allude to the laws in force in all Roman cities and express a mentality which coincides to a large extent to that of the Pompeians.

A general picture: towards emancipation
In contrast to the laws of other ancient cultures, Roman law provided that on the death of their father daughters could inherit their share of the estate on equal terms with sons. However, compared to males, females could not dispose of their property freely: when the *pater* died they were put into guardianship, at whatever age and for all of their lives (not only if they were under age like their male counterparts). However, during the last centuries of the Republic, apart from acquiring new rights (for example, that of inheriting from their husbands), women acquired greater patrimonial autonomy. The wars which had bathed the last few centuries of the Republic in blood had decimated the male population, so that an immense wealth was concentrated in the hands of orphans and women. In the absence of the men (occupied outside the cities in fighting or in administration of the conquered territories), women saw their condition change radically. At the time when Pompeii became a Roman colony,

Woman at the door. Stucco from Pompeii, House of Meleager. National Archaeological Museum, Naples

*Pearl and precious
stones earrings
and gold bracelets
in the form of snakes,
from Pompeii.
National Archaeological
Museum, Naples*

the Forum. Mamia had donated a temple to the city known as "Temple of the genius of the Emperor". Eumachia was no less generous than Mamia: in the years preceding the earthquake of 62 AD, she had donated a building in the Forum to the city, probably a wool market. Finally we should remember that the wealthy women of Pompeii were not all aristocrats: proof of which is given by the funerary monument built on Via dei Sepolcri, in the 1st century AD, by the freedwoman *Naevoleia Tyche*, whose image is carved on the tomb. Naevoleia had married *C. Munatius Faustus*, who had held a high priesthood and to whom an honorary post of decurion had been offered. Naevoleia had commissioned the funerary monument not only for herself and her husband, but also for their slaves, to whom they had granted their freedom (CIL X, 1030).

Women, business and work
In Pompeii many women participated in the financial and commercial life of the city, either by personally managing their family's wealth or by working, whether independently or for others. For example, we may take the case of Asellina, who sold hot drinks in a *thermopolium* on Via dell'Abbondanza, and as a famous electoral manifesto painted on the walls of her tavern shows, invited her customers to vote for Caio Lolio Fusco as a candidate for *duovir aedibus sacris publicis procurandis* (CIL IV 7863). Other women designated as *Asellinae* signed the manifesto with her, but their relationship with Asellina is uncertain. According to some scholars, they were slave-waitresses. Others believe that they were prostitutes, an idea which appears to be totally unfounded. Clearly, commercial enterprises of some importance were managed by women, who were not only active business women but also engaged in politics,

women were essentially free, often extremely rich (if they belonged to the upper classes) and psychologically and socially emancipated over all.

The situation in Pompeii:
money and powerful women
The most well-to-do women in Pompeii (or at least some of them) possessed splendid villas in the vicinity of the city, like the famous *Villa Oplontis*, probably the property of Sabina Poppaea, wife of Nero. Other women held public offices as priestesses and participated so actively in the life of the city that they received public honours on their death. This happened, for example, to Mamia, a priestess from an ancient Samnitic family, and Eumachia, daughter of a wine producer who exported his wares to Phoenicia, Spain, Africa and Greece. A tomb was built for Mamia on land donated by the city for reasons which are explained in an inscription found in

and whose electoral support evidently carried some weight (as we shall see more clearly in the next paragraph). In any case, these women were not emancipated by work: it would be an historical error to interpret feminine work in itself as a sign of freedom (including prostitution, sometimes considered as a form of emancipation). In Rome employment was not a victory for anyone. On the contrary, it was a necessity for some women and many men who had to struggle to survive. The ideal, during the Roman age was "*otium*" (idleness), which at that time had no negative connotation. *Otium* was a privilege of the powerful, those who lived off their estate, who had no need to conduct business, which was known as *negotium* (from *nec-otium*, =not idleness). Still, this should not prevent us from emphasising that the number of working women was very high in Pompeii and that employment conferred a certain independence on many of them, both financial and social.

Women and politics
Although women did not have the right to vote, Pompeian women followed political events attentively and participated actively in electoral campaigns, by inviting their fellow citizens to vote for this or that candidate. From about 2500 electoral manifestos discovered, only 30% are signed. Among these 52 were signed by women in favour of 28 different candidates. However, women's choices were the same as those of the general population. Indeed, not infrequently they signed the same manifestos as men did. Presumably they chose candidates on the basis of criteria similar to those of men, that is to say relationships with relatives, patrons, clients or allies. Information about the status of the women involved in these activities is provided by the names of the

signatories, amongst whom 24 different, gentilitial surnames testify to the *status* of *ingenua* (born free) of those who bore them. However, together with the Latin names (about half of the total) there are also non-Latin ones, and in general Greek names were a sign of servile origins. Therefore, even freedwomen participated in political life, in accordance with the high social status they could attain (as seen by the case of Naevoleia Tyche). From Asellina's manifesto we can also deduce that women of modest economic means, perhaps of servile origin, actively interested themselves in local politics.

Women and education
The women of Pompeii received a certain education according to the rules of the Roman and Romanised world. According to some scholars about 20 percent of the city's women knew how to read and write, a percentage considered to coincide with the number of the women belonging to the most important families (from the decurion class or that immediately below it). But

"Sappho". This small picture found in Pompeii in the 'Insula Occidentalis' is traditionally held to be a portrait of the famous Greek poetess. In fact it is probably a young Roman woman of high class, portrayed with a stylus and wax tablet, in the act of preparing to write. National Archaeological Museum, Naples

Gold, pearl and emerald necklace, from Pompeii. National Archaeological Museum, Naples

"Medea", fresco from Pompeii, House of the Dioscuri. National Archaeological Museum, Naples. This female figure is dressed in the traditional clothes of a Roman lady

in Rome education for women was not a privilege of the upper classes, nor was it limited to a basic cultural education. Even though our information is fragmentary, we know that in the 4th century BC a system of public instruction existed, probably carried out by itinerant teachers, and that this system was consolidated in the 3rd century. We also know that these schools were attended by children, both male and female, whose families could not afford to pay for a private tutor (as was the custom of the wealthiest families). Certainly, though, the level of education available to upper class women was greater – after reading, writing and counting in the elementary schools – we know that women of the upper classes took part in private lessons given by tutors together with the males in the family. Consequently they learnt literature (Latin and Greek) and some elements of rhetoric and law.

Clothing

Inside the home, men and women wore an item of clothing of the same name: the tunic, composed of two long pieces of wool, sewn together in the upper section and worn, by men, in direct contact with the skin. It was held around the waist by a belt. Whilst the male tunic reached the shins, the female one was longer and even covered the ankles. Women also wore a tunic against the skin (*tunica interior*, today called a vest), under or over which they tied a *fascia pectoralis* (the equivalent of a modern bra) also called *strophium* or *taenia* in Greek.

When they went out, however, men and women wore different clothes. Men wore a toga, a heavy garment of white wool, which was wrapped around the left arm allowing the right arm to be free. It had so many folds that it was difficult to put on. A slave was employed at night by the wealthy to prepare the folds of the toga which they would wear the following day.

In contrast, women wore a *stola*, a loose garment of wool, which reached their feet and which was tied at the waist by a belt. In the case of the women, the monotony of this clothing was relieved by use of different coloured materials together with ornaments and jewels, the number and variety of which depending on what the women could afford. Jewellery included rings, bracelets, earrings, bands, buckles, necklaces and ankle bracelets decorated with gold and precious stones. In fact, Roman women loved wearing jewellery, as shown by the paintings and exhibits from Pompeii.

Finally, when the normally temperate climate made it necessary, women wore a *palla* to protect themselves from the cold.

This was a loose cloak which replaced the more ancient *ricinium*, which covered the shoulders and even the head. Footwear, which was identical for men and women, consisted of *soleae*, similar to present day sandals, worn at home, and the *calcei*, for outdoors. Women's footwear was made of softer and more colourful leather (red and gold were very popular) and embellished with embroidery and precious stones such as pearls.

We should remember that Roman women had nothing similar to a hat. They went with their heads uncovered, and only because of the cold, or for decorum, if they were *matronae* (noble ladies) would they pull the edge of their *palla* over their heads.

Politics

The government of the city: the municipium and the Roman colony

The history of political institutions in Pompeii can be followed with precision from 80 BC, the year in which Pompeii became a Roman colony. Documentation relating to the previous period is very scarce: we know that at the time of the Samnite Wars (fought between 343 and 290 BC) Pompeii was part of a league of cities with headquarters at *Nuceria* (Nocera), and that this league fought against Hannibal as Roman allies. Of the government of the Samnite cities, during that age, little is known, only that they were governed by a supreme magistrate, called *meddix tuticus*, who it appears was also concerned with the administration of justice. The earliest reliable information regarding political life in Pompeii dates back to the 2nd century BC, when an increase in epigraphic documentation tells us that the city was governed by annually elected magistrates and by a council composed of ex-magistrates. This type of government changed following the participation of Pompeii in the so-called Social Wars, between 91 and 89 BC, which was fought against Rome by her Italic *soci* (allies) to obtain Roman citizenship.

After conquest by Roman troops, it appears that Pompeii became a municipality (*municipium*). In practice, this meant that the inhabitants of Pompeii, like all other *municipes*, acquired Roman citizenship, but as the etymology of *municipium* demonstrates,

(from *munera capere*, "acquiring duties") they acquired citizens' obligations – for example fiscal or military – but not rights. In short, inhabitants of municipalities effectively lost their political freedom. Rome allowed them a certain autonomy in local administration, in this case by a bench of four magistrates (*quattuoviri*) alongside of which was a *quaestor*. In addition, as in all municipalities, the possibility of exercising a certain jurisdiction autonomously, although somewhat limited, was also recognised in Pompeii, to which we will return later.

In 80 BC, things changed. In that year, in fact, Sulla founded the *Colonia Cornelia Veneria Pompeiorum* in Pompeii (The Colony of Pompeians under the auspices of Cornelius Sulla and of the goddess Venus) and this created a series of problems.

In ancient times a colony was not, as in modern times, a distant conquered territory, and together with its inhabitants, subject to the government of its conqueror. Rather, it was formed by a group of citizens who (originally for military reasons, and subsequently for demographic ones) went, following the orders of a magistrate, to found a new city, which was considered as a detached branch of the fatherland. When this colony was set up in an already inhabited place (as in the case of Pompeii), the two groups with different

cultures and political institutions found themselves forced into cohabitation. It would seem that in this particular case, Sulla (who at the end of the war in the Orient had to settle his ex-soldiers) quartered his most faithful followers and some of their families in Pompeii (between five and six thousand according to the most credible estimates), by confiscating the necessary land and housing.

The effects of this event have been hotly debated. It is obvious, however, that they were in some measure traumatic and that they altered the local equilibrium at least for some time. Certain references in the sources have led us to believe that measures were taken which led to the original inhabitants not only losing their right to vote (*suffragium*), but, furthermore, their right to move around freely within the city itself (*ambulatio*). However, more recent research tends to exclude that this actually happened. On the contrary, epigraphic documentation shows that with the arrival of the colonists, after an initially problematic phase, during which the original inhabitants were excluded from public office, there was no definitive change in the ruling classes. In the course of a few decades cohabitation between the old and new inhabitants settled down and fresh proof of the easing of the relationship between the two groups is

Equestrian statue representing Marcus Nonius Balbus, one of the most eminent personalities in Herculaneum. At least another ten statues were erected in his honour in the city, according to existing documentation. National Archaeological Museum, Naples

Electoral propaganda, painted on the wall of Via dell'Abbondanza in Pompeii

found in the homologation of the old and new magistracy. The municipal *quattuoviri* were replaced with two pairs of *duoviri* (duumvirs). The most important of these, composed of *duoviri iure dicundo* were concerned with the administration of justice. These *duoviri* were also expected to convene and preside over the assemblies (who elected the magistrates) and a council of citizens (*ordo decurionum*) composed of a hundred former magistrates. The other pair of *duoviri* (also defined as *duoviri viis aedibus sacris publicis procurandis*) were entrusted with the maintenance of the roads, sacred and public buildings, the markets and public order. After 45-40 BC these *duoviri* were called "aediles" (*aediles*). From some inscriptions it may be deduced that they exercised a limited jurisdiction, probably in the field of buying and selling and of the markets, similar to that held by the "edili curuli" in Rome. Finally, with the objective of producing a census of the citizens and updating the census list, every five years certain *duoviri* called *quinquennales* (nominated every five years) were elected in place of the *duoviri iure dicundo.* These magistrates, whose functions were similar to those of the Roman censors, were concerned with the updating of the roll of decurions and had the power to exercise a certain control over public morality by issuing a writ for any behaviour considered incorrect. The meetings of the council of decurions were held in the Curia, which occupied the central section of the southern side of the Forum. The seat of the *duoviri* was situated to the east of the Curia, and to its left that of the aediles. (monument 4).

Elections and electoral manifestos

Each year, with the need to elect new magistrates, the entire population of Pompeii participated actively in the election campaigns. The merits and demerits of the various candidates (so-called because they wore a special white toga called *candida* during the run-up to the elections) were discussed animatedly in all meeting places from the streets to the taverns and in the public baths, and electoral manifestos invited citizens to vote for the different candidates. In contrast to modern day manifestos, the Pompeian ones, called *programmata*, did not consist of paper documents but of exhortations written directly on walls. It is thanks to this characteristic that they have come down to us and can be read today. Lacking designated spaces for election propaganda, each inhabitant of the city utilised a part of the walls of his home or part of a building at his disposition. The walls were prepared for this purpose by a whitewashing of lime, entrusted to a *dealbator* (whitewasher), and then at night, the electoral manifesto was written by the light of an oil lamp held by a *lanternarius.* But there were also those who boasted on the manifesto that they had done everything or almost everything by themselves, as for example Mustius the laundry worker (CIL IV 3529, in the Vicolo degli Scienziati near the House of the Vettii). After having called for votes for Marcius Rufus as "duoviro giusdiscente", Mustius wrote: "Mustius the laundry worker votes for him and has whitewashed (the walls); he wrote this alone, without other companions" (*Mustius fullo facit et dealbat scripsit unicus sine reliquis sodalibus*).

The *programmata*, therefore, were not the work of the candidate. A candidate would spread propaganda using any means to make himself popular and would manage public relations carefully. For example, to give all his constituents the feeling that he remembered them, he would use a slave on purpose called *nomenclator*, whose function was to whisper the name of every passer-by encountered who greeted the candidate. But the electoral manifestos were not part of the propaganda that a candidate could dispense personally, in the sense that they were not signed by him (even though sometimes solicited by him), but signed by relatives, friends, various supporters, and sometimes by entire professional associations. The *fullones* (laundry workers) for example, asked for votes for Olconius Priscus as duumvir (CIL IV, 7164, at the entrance to the Fullery of Stefanus); the *aurifices* (goldsmiths) supported the candidature of Caius Cuspius Pansa for aedileship (CIL IV 710, on the walls of the building of Eumachia); the *clibanari* (pastry vendors) backed Trebius Valente as aedile candidate (CIL IV 677, in the Vicolo del Balcone pensile); the *muliones* (muleteers) wanted to elect Caius Julius Polybius as duumvir (CIL IV 113, in Via Consolare); "the fruit merchants want M. Enium Sabinum as aedile" (*M. Enium Sabinum aedilem pomarii rogant*) (CIL IV, 180), and so on. Sometimes groups of people who frequented the same places regularly would ask for a vote, as, for instance, the *spectaculi spectantes* (spectators of the amphitheatre) who supported Olconius Priscus as duumvir (CIL IV; 755885, near the Amphitheatre). Usually on the manifesto, the name of the candidate would be followed by an indication of the public office for which he was campaigning, and then contained an invitation to vote for him, often abbreviated to a few letters such as OVF (*Oro Vos Faciatis*, "we beg you to do it", in other words to vote). For example, in CIL IV; 336 (via di Nola) we can read: *Sallustium Capitonem aedilem o.v.f. caupones facite* (Vote for Sallustium Capitonem as aedile, Tavern Keepers - vote for him.)

The qualities of the candidate, on their part, were often synthesised by a few letters such as DPR (*Dignum Rei Publicae*, "worthy of the Republic"); VB (*virum bonum*, an honest man); or written in full, *dignissimus* (most worthy), *probissimus* (most upright),

optimus (excellent) and other such adjectives which indicated the qualities evidently considered necessary to hold public office. But apart from recommendation for honesty and prestige, there were those who were recommended as candidates because they lived a reserved life (*verecunde vivens*) such as, for example, Caius Cuspius, aedile candidate (CIL IV 7201) or because they were *sanctissimus* (highly virtuous). The *programmata* can be divided into two categories: those called *antiquissima*, dating to the period

Statue of Marcus Holconius Rufus in armour, from Pompeii. The military costume alludes to the office of 'tribunus militum'. The inscription below the statue reminds us that he was a duumvir 'iure dicundo' five times and twice a quinquennial duumvir. National Archaeological Museum, Naples

The Forum and the Temple of Jupiter in Pompeii in a 19th century engraving

preceding the settlement of the Sullan colony (80 BC) and those called *recentiora*, dated to the last seventeen years of Pompeii. Some of the latter, in contrast to the former, were signed by women, such as that of Asellina quoted earlier (CIL IV 7863).

The administration of justice

In contrast to the situation in other cities, no legislative documents relating to the local jurisdictional system have been found in Pompeii. Our information on this subject, therefore, derives in part from epigraphs and in part from information obtained from the laws regarding the organisation of other Roman cities.

As we have already stated, both civil and criminal jurisdiction was exercised by the *duoviri*. In criminal matters, these magistrates had a wide range of competence; for example, they judged decurions accused of "unworthiness", people who were election candidates without the required qualifications, those accused of *ambitus* (incorrect behaviour during the elections), of peculation (robbery or misuse of public

funds) and possibly also of murder. In short, municipal magistrates had a general criminal competence, which excluded only those crimes which endangered security and the public order of Rome (more specifically *perduellio*, that is high treason).

In the exercise of this jurisdiction, the *duoviri* had the power to inflict severe punishments, such as exile from Italic territory. Finally, among their duties, was the application of these sentences including execution of those sentenced to death, but only in cases where the condemned person was either a slave or a foreigner. In civil matters, the authority of the *duoviri* was limited to lawsuits whose value did not exceed 15,000 sestertii. For trials involving defamatory convictions, the limit was lowered to 10,000 sestertii.

Between politics and justice: jurists and lawyers

The administration of justice was an extremely important occasion in city life. In trials, in fact, not only were the interests of the various parties at stake, but also the political careers of people who, whilst not personally involved in the lawsuit, contributed directly or indirectly to the decision, in the role of *iurisconsulti* (jurisconsults, jurists) or as lawyers. Here it is timely to clarify that in the Roman world jurists and lawyers did not have the same role. The jurist had the task of interpreting the law, that is explaining how and when legal rules should be applied. More precisely he gave advice (*responsa*), on request, which identified the appropriate regulation to apply to each specific case. Custom required that a jurist be available to the public from the early hours of the morning, in the atrium of his home, where the consultation took place in the presence of people who assisted in the hope of learning the art of law, who could thus acquire a certain degree of popularity to obtain a sufficient number of voters to embark on a political career. A lawyer (*orator*), on the other hand, did not give advice, but assisted the parties in the course of the trial. His function, nevertheless, was different from that of a modern day lawyer. In the Roman world the legal profession was not remunerated. It was a civil function, that by law (*lex Cincia*, of 204 B.C.) had to be practised without compensation (Tac., *Ann.*, 1, 5, 3). This rule (which turned into the custom of donating gifts to lawyers) was a clear indication of the civil-political connotation of this profession and it is no co-incidence that the most important politicians in ancient Rome trained as lawyers.

It was only following the advent of the principate that the legal profession separated from the complex of political affairs, to become a profession in its own right, for which a practising lawyer could claim financial compensation; even though this should not exceed 10,000 sestertii, as established by Claudius (Tac., *Ann.*, XI, 7,8). Pompeii witnessed the beginning of this transformation, which, however, never diminished the prestige of the legal profession.

The administration of justice took place in the *Basilica* and lawyers pronounced their address from the podium, a well preserved example of which can be admired in Pompeii (*The Monuments*, 4).

The emperor Tiberius as a priest, statue in the National Archaeological Museum, Naples

The economy

Agricultural Production

Pompeii owed its thriving economy to
particularly favourable environmental
conditions, the most important of which
was the extraordinary fertility of the
Campanian plain. Fruit and vegetables of
every type were cultivated in the soil
around Pompeii. Columella spoke of the
importance of the cabbages and onions of
Pompeii (*De re rust.*, X, 133, XII, 10, 1)
and Cato revered the figs of Herculaneum
(*De agri cult.*, VIII, 1). But the real wealth
of the area came from the extensive
harvesting of grapes and olives. In Pompeii
and its surroundings various types of wine
were produced deriving from different
grapes: *Amineo, Pompeiana, Vennuncula*
and *Holconia*; and the wines of good

quality produced were *Vesuvinum* or
Vesvinum and *Pomeianum*, a famous wine
which, according to Pliny, only improved
with age and caused headaches (Pliny,
N.H., XIV, 70).

Of extreme agricultural importance, the
grapevines had even penetrated inside
the walls of the city. Excavations have
revealed extensively cultivated areas
inside Pompeii, especially in the vicinity
of the Amphitheatre (the south-eastern
area). There were many taverns with
adjoining vineyards which allowed their
hosts to sell their own produce; but also
many private houses had their own
kitchen gardens with fruit trees and vines
which allowed each family to produce
sufficient wine for its own needs and a
part may have been for sale. Nevertheless,
the quantity of wine produced from the
urban vineyards must have been limited
and the Pompeians brought in wine from
the surrounding countryside. Two
paintings depict the wine *cullei*, large
wineskins made of ox leather, which were
brought into the city in carts. These
wineskins were then pierced and the wine
decanted into amphorae. Arriving in these
skins, the wine could also be poured
directly into the small *dolia* which can still
be seen encased in shop counters (20).
One thing is certain; it was no mystery that
the Pompeians loved drinking, as revealed
by a graffiti in which we read: *Avete, utres
sumus* (Cheers! We drink like wineskins).

Industry

Not all the wine from the Vesuvian
region was consumed locally, and its
export constituted an important source

of income for Pompeii. Wine amphorae from Pompeii have been found, not only in other parts of Italy, but also in France, Spain, Africa, Corsica, Germany and England. The production of wine and oil, whilst providing the principal wealth of the city, was not, however, the only economic activity in the region. There was a flourishing ceramics industry: *dolia* and amphorae were made which were essential for the exportation of wine and other products, and also tiles, oil lamps and porcelain were produced.

Pompeii was also famous for its textile industry and the guilds of craftsmen connected with this sector played an important part in political life.

The working of raw wool and its transformation into finished products was undertaken in different workshops. The beating and washing of the raw wool took place in the *officinae lanifricariae* where the wool was boiled in leaden boilers to eliminate residues of fat; whilst in the *officinae textoriae* the clean wool

was spun onto looms, mainly by women, and transformed into clothes. Dying of both old and new cloth took place in the *officinae tinctoriae*; and finally there were the real laundries (*fullonicae*) where garments were washed and, if white, bleached (19). Human and animal urine were amongst the most important substances used for washing (camel urine was particularly sought after and expensive) (Pliny, *N.H*, XVII, 46; XXVIII, 66, 91, 174).

In addition, there were also workshops for the production of footwear. Leather was tanned in the *officinae coriariorum*; and footwear was produced or repaired in the *officinae sutoriae*. Other workshops existed for the preparation of dyes; and there were shops which produced objects in ivory and metals. There were numerous craftsmen including marble workers (*marmoratii*), carpenters (*fabri lignarii*) mosaic craftsmen (*musivarii*); goldsmiths and gemstone cutters (*gemmarii*).

Roman balance with a weight in the form of the bust of Mercury, from Pompeii. National Archaeological Museum, Naples

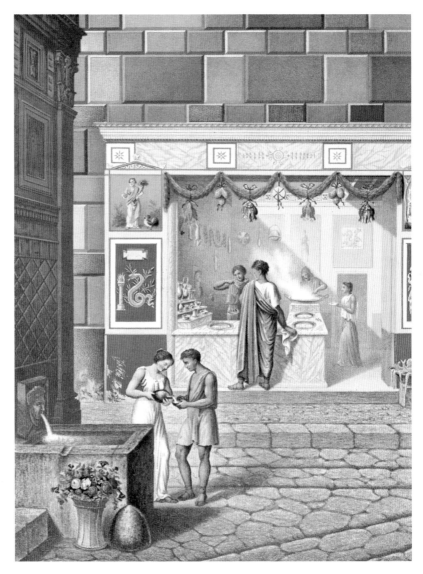

A shop in a street of Pompeii, in a 19th century reconstruction

Particularly important amongst the industries of Pompeii was the production and sale of *garum*, one of the most characteristic ingredients of the Roman cuisine. *Garum* was a famous sauce obtained by crushing fish in salt and it constituted the principal condiment used to flavour many dishes. There were various types of *garum*, depending on the quality of the fish used and its method of preparation (tuna, mackerel and moray eels were amongst the best quality; whilst anchovies were used for less refined sauces).

A particularly good quality *garum*, which was much sought after by Roman gourmets, was produced in Pompeii. Finally, it would seem that Pompeii was noted for its top quality olive presses which were made from volcanic stone. Cato (*De Agric.*, 22, 3; 135, 2) found it convenient to buy an olive press in Pompeii to take to his villa in Molise, despite the high costs of transportation.

Commerce

Commerce contributed in large measure to the economy of Pompeii and was

particularly favoured by the geographical location of the city. Strabo (V, 4, 8) notes that Pompeii functioned as a maritime outlet for the commercial activities of the rich centres of the Campanian hinterland: Nola, Nocera and Acerra. The exact site of the port of Pompeii is still under discussion, not least because the ancient line of the coast has not been clearly demarcated. The export of wine constituted the most important commercial enterprise of Pompeii. There was also a thriving wholesale woollen industry, which was probably carried out in the Building of Eumachia (5), and a prospering food industry. The *macellum* (7), was a market specialising in the sale of meat and fish. In one of his plays Plautus listed all the types of meat found in the *macellum:* lamb (*agnina*), beef

(*bubula*), veal (*vitulina*) and pork (*porcina*). Poultry bred in aviaries was also sold at the market. The fish trade consisted principally of red mullet, sole, dory, dentex, turbot, and sturgeon as well as crustaceans and molluscs. Cereals and pulses were sold in another market, the *forum olitorium*, the Forum Granary or "vegetable market"(8), which was also situated in the Forum, on the side opposite the *macellum*. The construction of these huge markets demonstrates the civic administration's intention to exercise a check over the populations' food supplies, and over the quality and pricing of consumer goods. The markets, which were the property of the city, were administered and supervised by local magistrates, the aediles. They looked after the smooth-running of the markets and

Procession of carpenters, fresco from Pompeii. National Archaeological Museum, Naples

Relief representing a tinker's shop, from Pompeii, Shop VI, 7, 8-9. National Archaeological Museum, Naples

'Placentarius', itinerant peddler of 'placentae', i.e. buns. This bronze statuette was probably used as a tray. From Pompeii, House of the Ephebus

oversaw the enforcement of existing regulations, such as that which required traders to bring their goods to market at dawn or during the night to avoid traffic congestion in the city.

The *macellum* and the *forum olitorium* did not supply all the city's food requirements. There were numerous shops run by private entrepreneurs throughout the different districts of the city which produced fresh supplies of bread, pastries, vegetables and fruit. More than thirty bakeries have been found corresponding to the type belonging to *Popidius Priscus* (12), in which all the different phases of baking were carried out, from the milling of the wheat to the production of bread and cakes.

Shops, taverns, inns and workshops played an important part in the economic and social life of the city. Their surprisingly high number (about six hundred) constitute particularly interesting data when compared to the number of houses (a little more than eight hundred) and the size of the population (around ten thousand) and it is this proliferation which gave the city its distinctive commercial character.

Architectural typology of the shops

Shops are easily recognisable from their typology. They were characterised by a long aperture onto the street, which generally corresponded to the total width of the shop. The aperture had a threshold made of travertine or lavic stone, furrowed with a long central groove, which allowed a long, wooden shutter to slide along and fold back during the day. These shops might also have a backroom or mezzanine, accessible from the inside (*pergula*), destined as the home of the owner. Premises designated as public eating places (*cauponae, thermopolia*) were characterised by a stonework counter covered with marble in which the *dolia* were encased, the large amphorae used to hold hot drinks, vegetables, dried or smoked foods. There was often a stove at the end of the counter to cook food or to heat water, which, especially in winter, was used to dilute wine. Some of these eating places often had one or more rooms inside, sometimes furnished with the large tricliniums used for the most important patrons to eat their meals on couches, whilst the less important clients ate seated on benches. The number of these eating places, about two hundred, might seem excessive when compared to those in other ancient cities, such as Ostia (where there were only about forty). This number was probably justified by the presence of a large workforce employed from outside the city to assist in the reconstruction of Pompeii after the earthquake of 62.

Bakeries

There were numerous *pistrina*, the ovens used for the baking of bread and cakes. There were about thirty establishments of this type in Pompeii, almost all containing three or four mills. The mills were made from lavic stone, comprising a fixed block (*meta*) and a moving part (*catillus*) which was turned manually by workmen or with the help of donkeys. This explains why the courtyards were always paved with basalt flagstones, similar to those found in the streets. There was also a table where flour was kneaded into dough and an oven for baking. Many of these establishments had an adjoining area for sales, to enable them to carry out the entire operation from the milling of wheat to the sale of the finished products.

In ancient times bread was considered a basic foodstuff as it is now. However, it was particularly hard due to the poor quality of the flour and the lack of yeast, which if preserved too long went off. For this reason bread was rarely eaten fresh; it was consumed by dipping it in wine, oil and soup. The Romans were also familiar with a more refined type of bread and types made with spices, milk, eggs, honey and oil. There were two types of loaves – a long one and a round one. The latter had four or eight cross-shaped incisions which allowed it to be broken up easily. Different shaped loaves have been noted, such as that alluded to by Martialis in an epigram which admonishes *Lupus* for allowing his lover to become fat by eating obscene-shaped bread (IX, 2). There were also different types of "pizza": a soft one (*artolaganum*) and a crunchy one (*tracta*).

Other types of shops and workshops

Apart from eating establishments a number of shops existed including rag and bone vendors (*veterarii*), greengrocers (*tabernae pomariae*), sellers of glassware, particularly vases (*taberna vitraria*), silverware (*argentariae*) and perfume vendors (*tabernae unguentariae*). *Officinae oleariae* and *vinariae* also existed, which apart from the retailing of oil and wine, produced their own oils and wines, as testified by the machinery found there, and they also produced *garum*, the famous fish sauce mentioned earlier.

Itinerant trading

Itinerant trading was another commercial aspect of Pompeii. To this end stalls were set up in the squares, under porches and arcades, or in the streets protected by tents. Obviously the most popular sites were those which were well-frequented: around the Forum, near the thermal baths and the theatres or Amphitheatre, as shown by the famous fresco depicting the Amphitheatre of Pompeii during the notorious riot between the Pompeians and Nocerines, where the artist realistically painted in wooden market stalls or portable tents; or the series of frescoes representing scenes of life in the Forum of Pompeii.

There is documentary evidence of the existence of city markets (*nundinae*) which represented retail outlets for the *surplus* agricultural products of farmers from the hinterland and also places to purchase goods which the farmers were not able to produce themselves. Thanks to the *Indices Nundinarii*, lists indicating the days on which the markets were held in the different cities, we know that market day in Pompeii was on a Saturday.

Religious life

An open religion

The religious life of the inhabitants of Pompeii was very intense and complex. In their temples and in their homes they honoured divine entities of different origins and types; the cults of ancient indigenous gods were followed alongside the veneration of Greek, Roman and Oriental gods. From the Greek-Roman Pantheon they worshipped firstly Jupiter (*Iuppiter*, or "Jupiter the Father", corresponding to the Greek Zeus) who together with his wife, Juno (corresponding to the Greek Hera) and Minerva (the Greek Athena) formed the Capitoline triad, to whom they dedicated the greatest temple in the Forum of Pompeii (3).

The god Apollo was also very dear to the Pompeians, his local cult dates back to the 6th century BC and the most ancient temple of the city is dedicated to him (2). The cult of Venus, the goddess of love, was equally important, and she became the patroness of the city following the founding of the Sullan colony in the year 80 BC. She was worshipped in a temple in the south-eastern corner of the city which was built on an artificial terrace facing the sea. From here the goddess gave her protection to sailors and to the maritime trade which constituted one of the most important resources of the city (1).
Other divinities who enjoyed popularity were Bacchus (corresponding to the Greek Dionysus), the god of wine and lord of the intoxication it produced; and the Egyptian Isis, to whom numerous sanctuaries throughout Campania were dedicated.
From Augustus onwards, when the Emperors were deified, Pompeii became the centre of a fervent imperial cult, administered by a true hierarchy of priests and priestesses. Another interesting public cult was bestowed on the patrons of the family, the Lares (*Lares*), who were also considered protectors of the crossroads (*compita*) and in this capacity were honoured as *Lari Compitales* (from the Augustan period *Lari Augustales*).
Finally, we should remember that Roman piety was not limited to the worship of personified gods. Apart from the most important gods, conceived of and venerated in human form, there were beliefs in entities endowed with

incorporeal and magical powers, who lived inside objects, and to whom the Romans dedicated a cult which fell somewhere between a religion and magical practices. These forces, called *indigetes*, were propitiated with their special rites called *indigitamenta*, or when necessary kept away with 'deprecations', consisting of ritualistic gestures accompanied by magical curses.

Public worship, blood sacrifices and sacrificial banquets

In Pompeii, as in Rome, gods were the objects of both public and private worship. Public worship was celebrated in the city temples by priests and priestesses.

The most characteristic feature of the official Roman religion was its essentially political orientation. In fact, priesthood was considered a public office by the Romans, although of a specific nature, and above all religious life was conceived of as a political duty which all citizens were expected to perform scrupulously rather than as an interior relationship between the faithful and a god.

One of the most solemn moments in the celebration of public ritual was the

delivering of offerings to a god, in the course of an act called *sacrificium* (from *sacrum facere*, "to render sacred"). The most agreeable sacrifice for the gods was that of an animal and it was offered to them according to a meticulous series of ritual precepts. According to these precepts a herald would invite the congregation to maintain absolute silence, reciting the formula "favete linguis" (avoid words of bad omen). At this point a priest, with his head veiled, took a plate containing the *mola salsa* (a special mixture prepared by Vestal Virgins) and spread the mixture on the knife and head of the sacrificial animal (whence comes the verb "immolare" – to sacrifice), thereby initiating the main part of the ceremony, which consisted of the ritual killing of the animal and the subsequent division of its meat.

The meat was divided according to very precise rules which allowed no contraventions. The *exta*, that is to say the entrails of the victim, were destined for the gods, and were thus burnt in their honour. The remaining meat was divided between the different participants present at the rite, as if to assign a part of the victim to each one. The different cuts of meat, depending on whether their quality was considered superior or inferior, were allocated to each person according to the position he or she occupied in society or in the family. Finally, once the meat was cooked, it was eaten by the participants at a banquet which followed an inalterable order of precedence. At public sacrifices, the priests and senators ate in a separate place from the populace, who were given – when they were given anything at all – only small pieces of the poorest quality meat. At home the *paterfamilias* ate first in the centre of the dining room, and the women occupied the places furthest from the centre. In short, the sacrificial banquet (as in other ancient societies such as the Greek one) had, together with its religious value, an important social value. It served to remind each individual of his social standing and of what was appropriate behaviour, both within the family and in public life.

The mystical cults

The collective management of official religious life, which took place during the course of public festivals organised by the State, relegated secondary importance to contact between the faithful and their divinities. In response to the need for this contact and for direct communication with a god, which many people felt, a number of cults came into being and developed, which evaded state and domestic organisation, and which were conducted in private brotherhoods. Of these cults, those of Isis and Bacchus became well-known and widespread in Pompeii.

Isis

Isis was the goddess who consoled human suffering, and who promised happiness and salvation from every evil; whilst her divine husband, Osiris, promised resurrection of the dead. Other benefits were assured to the followers of Isis by Anubis, her mysterious servant with the head of a jackal.
The powers which Isis commanded were mysterious and terrifying, as was the myth which surrounded her. According to this myth, after desperately searching for the decimated body of her assassinated husband, Isis found it and recomposed it, but without its genitals which had been eaten by a fish in the River Nile. Being a witch, however, Isis was able to create a new member for Osiris, and thence gave birth to a son by him, who was called Horus by the Egyptians and Harpocrates by the Greeks.
However, the relationship between Isis and her son was a complex one. In fact, Horus, after attempting to rape his mother, beheaded her and replaced her

head with that of a cow. This bloody and alarming story was further complicated by the fact that Isis is said to have been a prostitute in Tyre for ten years. Consequently, the life of Isis undermined the impassable boundary constituting one of the bastions of State security in Roman mentality, that is to say, the division of women into two categories: those women destined for legitimate reproduction and those who were destined to satisfy men's diverse needs. Moreover, the worship of Isis was mystical, and the fact that it was secret, allowed rumours to spread that those who frequented her temple were prostitutes. In short, Isis endangered ancient values, and on numerous occasions the worried authorities intervened with severity to control the spread of the cult.
But the cult continued to remain popular and widespread. We need only remember that the Temple of Isis in Pompeii was one of the first buildings of worship to be restored following the earthquake of '62, and the Popidii family, who were given the honour of its reconstruction, received compensation by the concession of a seat in the local senate (17).
The worship of Isis, apart from daily rituals which required a morning invocation at sunrise and an afternoon sacrifice venerating the sacred water of the Nile, was celebrated by two festivals. The first festival called "The Navigation of Isis" (*Navigium Isidis*) took place on the 5th March. That day, according to an account by Apuleio, (*Metamorphosis* or *The Golden Ass*, XI, 7-11), the priest of the goddess, at the head of the procession of followers, brought an artistically-crafted small boat to the sea shore. Having purified it with water and sulphur, he dedicated it to the goddess, the patroness of sailors, so that she would protect the sea-faring voyages recommencing after the winter months. In contrast, the second festival, the *Isia*,

On the following page:
Bacchus, his body formed by a bunch of grapes, is represented against the background of a mountain, thought to be Vesuvius. The augural snake and other decorations are typical motifs of lararium paintings. The fresco comes from the house of the Centenary. National Archaeological Museum, Naples

was celebrated from the 13th to the 16th November, and commemorated the re-discovery of the body of Osiris.

Bacchus and the Bacchanalian revels

The cult of Bacchus had been propagated throughout the region of Pompeii and more generally Campania for some time, as confirmed by a story of Titus Livius, according to whom the Bacchanalian cult had been spread by initiative of the Campanian priestess Annia Paculla. Furthermore, the priestess had admitted men to the originally feminine cult and had transformed the initiation rites from the morning to the night-time.

Assuring the faithful an irrational escape from reality, the rites of Bacchus, which seemed to provide answers to otherwise unsolved questions, spread rapidly, undoubtedly favoured by the climate of unease and uncertainty produced by the great social changes of the 2nd century BC. As women and slaves also participated in this cult, rumours therefore began to circulate that promiscuous sexual encounters took place during the Bacchanalian revels and that the followers of the god were members of a dangerous secret sect (Liv., XXXIX, 12-13).

The authorities, always suspicious of what they could not control, took drastic measures, by approving, in 186 BC, a *senatus-consultum de bacchanalibus* (recorded in the *Corpus Inscriptionum Latinarum* I, 581). The *senatus-consultum* ordered the demolition of temples dedicated to the god, forbade the celebration of secret rites without the authorisation of the praetor and the

This beautiful mosaic signed by Dioskourides of Samos comes from the so-called Villa of Cicero, in Pompeii. It probably represents a witch preparing a love potion for clients. National Archaeological Museum, Naples

Bronze, votive hand from Herculaneum. National Archaeological Museum, Naples. The gesture of benediction with bent fingers is typical of the cult of the god, imported from Asia Minor to Rome through Greece. The seated figure represents the god Sabatius

Death memento, mosaic from Pompeii, House-shop I, 5, 2. National Archaeological Museum, Naples. This motif, designed to remind table-companions of the vanity of terrestrial objects, decorated a triclinium

approval of the Senate, and established the death penalty as the punishment for anyone violating this provision, as was the case for any men or women who celebrated religious rites in groups of more than five people. To ensure that the *senatus-consultum* was respected outside Rome, the Senate distributed copies "throughout Italy", as Livius noted. But all of this had no apparent effect in Pompeii, and the cult continued to be practised undisturbed, possibly due to a special dispensation. The Dionysian frieze preserved in the Villa of the Mysteries in Pompeii provides extraordinary documentation of the devotion to Bacchus and to the revelries held in the god's honour. (25).

Private worship and belief in the afterlife

Private worship was celebrated in the homes of the *paterfamilias*, who acted as high priests. There were numerous

divinities who were worshipped at home. Amongst the most important were the goddesses Venus and Vesta. But the most popular family worship remained that dedicated to their dead ancestors, whose souls, like those of all who had passed on, were believed to live on after corporeal death, but in a form that in no way resembled that of the Christian belief.

In the Roman world the dead were named *Manes*. These Manes were entities which, although continuing to exist in another world, had no individuality and were lost in a mixture of benevolent and malevolent forces. For example, the souls of hanged men were considered malevolent entities, as were the dead who had received no funeral rites (called *iusta*, the proper, rightful things).

On every occasion both small and large offerings were made in honour of those considered the benevolent dead, who in relationship to their relatives were called the *Lares*. For instance, since it was believed that the Lares resided in the floors, there was a daily offering of the crumbs of food which had fallen on the floor during the course of a meal, and which consequently were not swept up. There were also feast days held in their honour, named *Feralia* and *Parentalia*, during which a communal meal was eaten, at which the images of the defunct were present. These images were represented by wax masks of the dead which were kept by each household.

Magical-religious rites and superstitions

The Pompeians used every possible means to propitiate good luck. Amongst these were the "mani pantee", namely the bronze hands with three fingers raised (the thumb, index and middle finger) and with the ring finger and small finger bent over in the gesture of the "Latin benediction". In the palm of these hands, in the space between the index and middle finger, was a seated image of the god Sabatius, with other symbols

connected to other deities, such as a snake, a toad, a beetle, a pine-cone and a bird. In line with the wrist, inside the elliptic arch, was the image of a woman and child, which suggested that these "mani pantee" were amulets intended to protect maternity and breast-feeding. However, the most widespread amulet in Pompeii was the erect phallus, symbol of virility and fertility. The phallus, represented by a large number of graffiti and bas-reliefs, was used to decorate houses and the street corners of the city.

Funeral rites and funerals: the procession of ancestors

The complexity of rituals which accompanied the passage from life to

*The House of the
Coloured Capitals
in Pompeii, watercolour
by Giacinto Gigante,
detail. Astarita
collection, Capodimonte
Museum, Naples*

death began even before the dying drew
their last breath.

The Italic population, or at least those
whose customs and beliefs are known to
us, believed that the deceased returned
to the earth from whence they came.
Consequently, the critically sick (called
desperati, without hope) were laid on the
floor.

On the advent of death the relatives,
after having given a last kiss to their dead
relative, closed his eyes and proceeded
with the rite of the *conclamatio* (the
invocation of his name aloud) and
entrusted the preparation of the corpse
to the women of the household or to
men employed as undertakers
(*libitinarii*). The corpse was washed,
oiled, and underwent a treatment to
guarantee its preservation, it was then
dressed and laid out on a bed in the
atrium of the house for visitors to see.
Afterwards, a coin was placed under the
tongue for the ferryman Charon, who, it
was believed, under payment, bore the
souls of the dead to Hades, which was
reached by crossing a river.

On the established day and time, the
funeral procession (*pompa*) left the house
of the deceased, preceded and
accompanied by musicians playing a
variety of instruments, and followed by
praeficae, women who were paid to
scratch their cheeks and wail terrible
screams of pain.

However, the strangest and most striking
aspect of the funeral rite was
undoubtedly the presence of the
ancestors, named *maiores* ("the elders").
In fact, on the occasion of a funeral, the
wax masks of the deceased were
removed from the cupboards in which
they were kept and were worn during the
procession by their descendants who
most resembled them in height and
build. The ancestors therefore took part
in the funerals of their descendants and
served as a reminder that death did not
only involve an individual member of the
family. In fact death involved the entire
lineage in as much as it fused the
deceased to the community of ancestors,
who were the protectors of the lineage:
when an individual passed on the family
continued to exist.

Tombs

In Pompeii, as in the entire Italic
territory, the two practices of cremation
and burial of corpses co-existed.
Regarding the city of Rome, the co-
existence of these two practices was
confirmed by a ruling of the Twelve
Tables, which in 450 BC, forbade the
cremation and burial of corpses inside
the city walls, that is inside the
pomerium.

This ruling, valid throughout the Roman
world, was also respected in Pompeii,
where tombs can be found outside the
city's boundary walls, along the streets
leading from the city gates: Porta Nola,
Porta Vesuvio, Porta Nocera and Porta
Herculaneum. Since tombs were
conceived of as the houses of the dead,
the defunct were buried together with
their clothes and the possessions which
they had utilised in their lifetimes: jewels
if they were women, toys if they were
children and arms if they were men.
Sometimes, these tombs were decorated
with bas-reliefs which recalled the lives
and occupations of the deceased, and
often a monogram was carved on the
monument, testifying to the conviction
that the dead continued to live on in
their tombs. This monogram consisted of
the four letters STTL, which stood for
Sit Tibi Terra Levis, or in other words
"may the earth be light upon you".

The city

Housing styles

Houses

Private buildings cover the largest urban area in Pompeii. The city therefore represents a privileged observatory for our knowledge of housing and its evolution over the course of several centuries.

The most ancient Pompeian houses, as for example the House of the Surgeon (IV, 1,10), date back to the 4th-3rd century BC, and demonstrate how from this early period the layout of the Italic-style house with an atrium had already been defined in its essential elements. These elements consisted of a door leading onto a short corridor (*fauces*) which opened onto the *atrium*, a spacious room in the centre around which other rooms were arranged; and a *hortus* (garden) which closed off the back of the house. The atrium was generally coverered by a roof with four pitches converging towards the inside (*compluvium*) to allow collection of rain water in a large pool situated in the centre of the floor (*impluvium*). This type of atrium was conceived to allow sufficient light into the house – which usually had no windows on the outside walls – and to conserve rain water which was essential for domestic needs particularly before the construction of the Augustan aqueduct, which provided houses with running water.

There were various types of atria. The most common in Pompeii was the Tuscan one which had no columns and roof pitches which converged towards the interior. The tetra style atrium had four supporting columns at each corner of the of the roof opening. The Corinthian atrium had more than four columns and the fourth type had no central opening.

The atrium was the heart of the primitive Italic house and according to certain authors of the ancient world the family would have eaten there. Its name derives from *ater* – dark, black – for the smoke produced in the hearth which blackened the walls (Servius, I, 6, 37). Located in the atrium was the lararium, a small altar dedicated to the Lares, the divinities which protected the house and the hearth. In this area the aristocratic families exhibited the *imagines maiorum*, the wax masks of their own ancestors. In the atrium good housewives would spend the day weaving.

In time the atrium of the Roman house, apart from discharging purely domestic services and functions, became the centre and symbol of social relations. Here important citizens, especially those who held public offices, received their supporters (*clientes*) who came to pay their daily respects (*salutatio matutina*), in exchange for gifts of money or food (*sportulae*) from the master of the house. The bedchambers (*cubicula*)) were laid out symmetrically around the atrium on either side with two halls (*alae*) on either side. At the end of the atrium, opposite the entrance, was a large room (*tablinum*), which either opened completely onto the atrium or was screened by curtains or wooden partitions. The family archive was originally located in the *tablinum* (Pliny,

N.H., XXXV, 2-7; Festo 490L), or, according to other hypotheses, the room held the marital bed (*lectus genialis*). Subsequently the *tablinum* was used essentially as a living or reception room, a type of extension of the atrium where the master of the house received his *clientes* and other guests.

Although the layout of the traditional Italic house remained the same, from the 2nd century BC the increasing wealth of the Pompeian nobility and the progressive assimilation of the Hellenistic culture led to the extension of the building complex. In particular the living areas were extended, which preserved an explicit reference to Hellenistic typology in the terminology used to describe them (*oeci, exedrae, diaetae* and *triclinia*). Even the *hortus* was transformed into an artistically designed garden, surrounded by an arcade with columns (*peristilium*) from which the principal living rooms looked out.

The extension of the house or villa constituted a distinctive sign of the wealthier classes, and a form of self-emulation of the owner. Some houses reached exceptional proportions, such as the House of the Faun or the House of Pansa, each of which covers an area of approximately 3000 square metres. The incentive to own ever more spacious and luxurious residences reinforced the tendency to construct dwellings beyond the walls as well, unrestricted by the city boundaries. First the southern and then the western slopes of Pompeii became the favourite areas to build residences in panoramic positions overlooking the sea. The spatial arrangement of these luxury houses is defined by a representational quarter and a servants' quarter. These two areas are easily distinguished by the fact that one passes from richly decorated areas to simple, rustic ones. The servants' quarters were usually decentralised with respect to the representational quarter, and were built

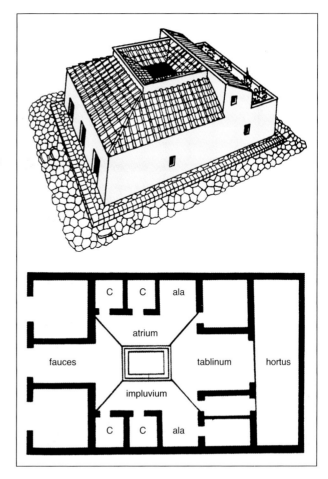

around the kitchen (*culina* or *coquina*) furnished with a stonework hearth consisting of a podium and a frontal recess to contain the firewood. The upper part was slightly hollowed out and covered with embers. Here the saucepans, usually of bronze, in which the food was cooked, were placed on metal tripods. Sometimes the kitchen also contained a small oven and a sink. The latrines were usually situated next to the kitchen as they utilised the same conduits for water supply. The stables, the warehouses to store foodstuffs and the slaves' lodgings were also located in the servants' quarters.

Some houses also contained an area dedicated to bathing, which reproduced the structure of the thermal baths on a small scale. The heated area of the baths

One of the columns of the Villa of the Columns in mosaics in a 19th century reproduction

The plan of a house 'with an atrium': plan and three-dimensional diagram

The atrium of a luxury
Pompeian house
in a 19th century
reproduction

The House of the
Coloured Capitals
in Pompeii
in a watercolour
by Giacinto Gigante.
Astarita collection,
Capodimonte
Museum, Naples

On page 50:
Wine press,
reconstruction of the
ram's head beam.
Pompeii, Villa
of the Mysteries

Drawing of a traditional
press from a Pompeian
farm. The roots were
left on the trunk of the
tree, which constituted
the lever, to act as
a counter-balance
(Adam 1989)

Drawing of an olive
press. A similar
grindstone was found
in Pompeii (Adam 1989)

was often situated adjacent to the kitchen so as to utilise the steam produced in the fireplace.

Apart from these grandiose *domus* more modest houses existed for the middle classes. A group of houses of this type has been identified in the south-eastern part of the city near the Amphitheatre (*Regiones* I and II), which seems to be the fruit of a homogenous plan dating to the time of the second Punic War (218-202 B.C.). These so-called 'terraced houses' had two floors to exploit the space above, thus solving the problem of residential urban density. A central room also constituted the focal point of these houses but it was arranged by width rather than by length, with no more than four annexed rooms and a small *hortus* at the back. The total area of these houses amounted to an average of about 200/250 square metres including both floors.

One other type of housing was the so-called *taberna*-house, which usually consisted of a frontal area used as a shop

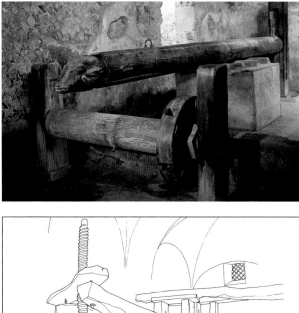

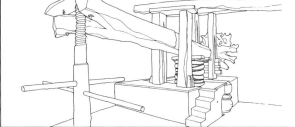

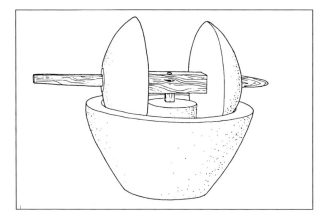

modest house, but especially after the earthquake of 62 – and probably as a consequence of the disastrous seismic effects on Pompeian housing – even luxurious apartments were rented out such as those situated above the Suburban Thermal Baths.

A number of announcements relating to the renting of different types of accommodation have been found on the walls of the House of Pansa: shops with lodgings above, luxury apartments and proper houses (CIL, IV, 138).

Elsewhere, on the exterior of the home of Julia Felix, an announcement was found advertising a small but luxurious thermal bath and other facilities for rent (*In praedis Iuliae Sp(urii) f(iliae) Felicis locantur balneum venerium et nongentum, tabernae, pergulae, caenacula, ex idibus Aug(ustis) primis in idus Aug(ustis)sextas, annos continuos quinque. S(i) q(uinquennium) d(ecurrerit) locatio) e(rit) n(udo) c(onsensu)*: "In the property of Julia, daughter of Spurius Felix, elegant thermal baths for refined people, shop with lodgings above and apartments on the first floor to let for five years from 1st August until 1st August of the sixth year. The contract may be renewed by mutual agreement after five years have passed" (CIL, IV, 1136).

Villas

Villa was the Latin term which described the type of residence situated outside the city walls and included both the so-called *villa rusticae*, the country farms designated for agricultural production, and the villas of *otium*, the luxurious residences built for relaxation and spending leisure time agreeably. From the 2nd century BC the Vesuvian area saw the rise of a conspicuous number of residential and country farm villas. In both cases the phenomenon was connected to the particularly favourable characteristics of Campania. The coastal section of the Phlegrean

with one or two rooms situated inside or on the upper floor (*pergulae*) used for accommodation. Lastly, there were houses or rooms for rent located on the upper floors of large residences (*cenacula*). Generally rented accommodation was reserved for the most humble classes of the population, who could not even afford to own a

Fields and Cape Campanella were, because of their natural beauty, the mildness of their climate, the health-giving properties of their mineral waters and the fascination of the Greek traditions, the ideal places to build a villa of *otium*. Here the wealthy Roman nobility dedicated themselves, far away from the bustle of urban life, to literature, philosophy and art. On the other hand, the region's hinterland with hills and valleys was particularly fertile and suitable for the cultivation of agricultural produce, which favoured the development of numerous country villas.

Rusticae villas and farming

In the area around Pompeii (Boscoreale, Boscotrecase, Scafati, Angri and Terzigno) about a hundred ancient country villas have been found. Usually they consist of medium-sized farms, distinguished by a residential quarter for the owner (*pars urbana*) and an area for farming with a servants' quarter (*pars rustica*). Due to the prolonged absence of the owner, these country villas were often entrusted to a farmer (*vilicus*). The labour force was largely composed of slaves, which limited the costs of production, but there were also free men and women working there. The most widespread and remunerative products were those from vineyards and olives. There was also extensive cultivation of fruit and cereals and the rearing of livestock. The running of these farm holdings involved considerable costs, especially for the use of machinery such as presses and mills. Some of this machinery has been preserved in good condition in Pompeii. The production of refined oils necessitated that the olive stones were first removed from the olives, so that the press did not break them and give a bitter taste to the oil. The machine used for the first pressing of the olives was the *trapetum* (an example of which can be

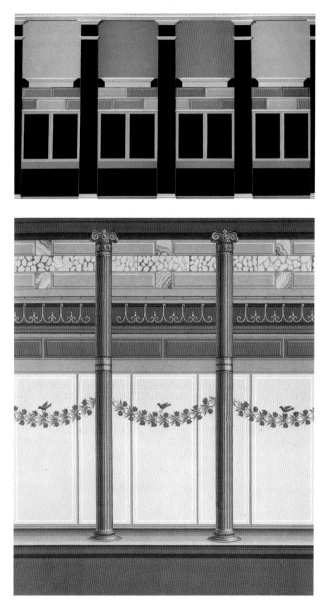

found in the Forum Granary, see monument 8). This consisted of a circular basin in lavic stone (*mortarium*) in which two hemi-spherical grindstones (*orbes*) turned, mounted on a cylindrical axis (*miliarium*). The presses were provided with a wooden bar used to turn the two grindstones that crushed the olives. The press (*torcular*), used to press both grapes and olives, consisted of a solid, wooden crossbar fixed at one end and pushed downwards by means of

An example of the First and Second Style of Pompeian painting

An example of the Third and Fourth Style of Pompeian painting

his guests often ended up assuming ever-greater importance. The fertility of the Vesuvian soil led to an increase in the number of residential villas in the area with annexed country quarters for farming. Examples of these are the so-called Villa of Poppaea in Oplontis, the Villa of P. Fannius Synistor in Boscoreale, the Villa of Agrippa Postumo and the Villa of the Mysteries in Pompeii.

The Villas of *otium*

As far as the villas of *otium* are concerned, the most important examples in the Vesuvian area relate to the 1st century BC and the 1st century AD. Ever more refined and grandiose dwellings became widespread in this period, which overtook urban residences in their luxury. The villas were enriched with peristyles, gardens, nymphaeums with scenographic water displays, Olympic-sized swimming pools, thermal baths, ornamental statues and ornate wall and floor decorations.

Decorations

Paintings and stuccoes

Apart from providing valuable information on domestic architecture, the houses of Pompeii and Herculaneum constitute the most important source of information on the evolution of Roman painting from the 2nd century BC to 79 AD. In fact, there is no other place in the world where such a large number of wall paintings and stuccoes are preserved. These materials are extremely delicate and only the unusual circumstance of the eruption of Vesuvius facilitated such particularly favourable conditions of preservation.

Apart from contributing to our knowledge of Roman painting, these findings provide valuable documentation of Greek painting. In fact almost all Greek paintings have

a winch with an arm lever, which crushed the grapes – and the olives – contained in baskets. A few olive presses have been found in Pompeii; a restored sample is in the so-called oil workshop (VII, 4, 24-25) and comes from house VII, 14, 14.

Wine production essentially needed a *torcularium* and a wine store, an open area where the wine fermented in terracotta containers (*dolia*), which were partially buried in the ground and arranged in parallel rows. Two wine presses can be seen in The Villa of the Mysteries (monument 25).

Even in these country villas, however, the quarter reserved for the owner and been lost, as have the majority of the wall decorations of Hellenistic cities. Pompeian painting reproduces and re-elaborates elements of Greek-Hellenistic art in the Italic style and is therefore fundamental to our acquaintance with this art form. We owe both the first attempt to classify Pompeian Painting according to the famous four styles and the establishment of a relative chronology to August Mau. This classification is still in use, although the system has been completed and integrated.

The *First Style*, or structural style, was found in Pompeii from the 2nd century BC to the beginning of the 1st century AD. It consists of the imitation of blocks or slabs of coloured marble in stucco that decorated the exterior of Hellenistic houses. The most representative examples of this style are preserved in the House of the Faun and the House of Sallustius.

The *Second Style* in Pompeii was probably due to the stimulus of Roman colonisation (80 BC). It constitutes an evolution of the previous style, in which the stucco relief is reproduced in painting. In the initial phase the decorative structure is quite simple, but soon after it becomes more complex, the wall 'opens up', giving an illusion of architectural perspective. Through arches and painted windows in the upper part of the walls, objects unfold on different planes (not always logical from the point of view of perspective) such as small temples, columns, walls and gardens, imagined as if they were situated beyond the room. It is current opinion that the illusionism of the Second Style was inspired by ornate theatrical scenography and monumental Hellenistic architecture. The most representative examples of this style are to be found in the oldest nucleus of the Villa A of Oplontis (Torre Annunciata). Another artistic expression of this style is found in the huge, figurative frescoes

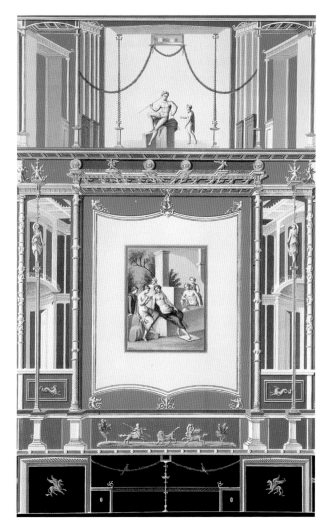

of the Villa of the Mysteries and the Villa of Boscoreale. In these frescoes the illusionary element is marginal and models deriving from the great Greek paintings prevail.

The *Third Style* developed from the Augustan age (the last twenty years of the 1st century BC) to the age of Claudius (about the middle of the 1st century AD) and is connected to Augustan classicism. The illusionary element completely disappears to give way to a purely pictorial reality. The walls are divided cleanly into the three sections – the skirting board, the middle and the upper walls. At the centre of the middle section there is usually a

Gold lamp with two necks, from the Temple of Venus in Pompeii. National Archaeological Museum, Naples

Tripod with satyrs, from the House of Julia Felix, Pompeii. National Archaeological Museum, Naples

mythological painting or sacred idyll; the side sections are emphasised by columns, vegetable stalks or candlesticks. In the upper section, usually on a pale background colour, slender architectonic elements are represented accompanied by vine shoots and garlands. Beautiful examples of this style can be found in the Villa of Agrippa Posthumus in Boscotrecase, the House of Marcus Lucretius Fronto (V, 4, 11), the House of the Orchard (1, 9, 5) and the Imperial Villa.

The Fourth Style is the most prominent in Pompeii, since it developed in the middle of the 1st century AD and was still in vogue at the time of the eruption. In addition, given that the earthquake of 62 (and perhaps not only that) had damaged numerous houses and public buildings in the city, many of the most ancient frescoes had been replaced with new decorations in the Fourth Style. The walls are always rigidly divided into three, and the middle section presents an alternation of wide panels and architectonic foreshortening in which the taste for an articulated and superimposed perspective re-emerges, but without the illusion of a reality beyond the walls as in the Second Style. The central panel still remains the site of a mythological painting, whilst small scenes (landscape or still life), or flying figures (cupids, representations of the four seasons etc.) are painted in the side panels. A stucco frame of lotus flowers and palm groves often crowns the upper section, articulated by niches in perspective connected by vine shoots, garlands or carpet borders. The tone of the colours is warmer and brighter and the effect of the colouring is emphasised by the combination of different backgrounds in yellow, black, red or sky-blue.

In this period the custom of lining walls in stucco came back into fashion. Stucco was most widely used on ceilings, but in the last period of the city's existence it was used on walls liberally and in different ways, both by itself (the Palaestra of the Stabian Baths), and in combination with painting (The House of Meleager, the Suburban Baths), increasing the effect of depth created by pictorial means with the size of the relief. Up to this point the 'cultured' style of painting examined is that inspired by models taken from Hellenistic derivation. But there is another type of painting in Pompeii, called 'popular', which reproduces events connected to real life. These are the paintings of the Lararia and the shop signs representing crafts and occupations, religious processions, erotic scenes, tavern scenes and gladiatorial images. Although the technique used is hasty and careless and

often lacks interest in perspective and proportions, these paintings nevertheless have a great freshness of expression and constitute invaluable evidence of the daily life of the city.

Floors and mosaics
The most ancient floors in Pompeii consist of a simple covering of mortar mixed with crushed tiles (cocciopesto) or a compound of crushed volcanic stone ("lavapesta"). Sometimes chips or tesserae of white or coloured limestone supported this material and were inserted in bulk or according to a geometric design. During the period in which the painting of the Second Style became widespread we can find the first mosaic floors embellished with black and white geometric designs. The floor could be enriched by a central picture (emblema) with mythological scenes, made from tiny coloured tesserae (House of Melander). During the period of the Third Style the emblema disappeared from mosaic floors to be replaced by a repertoire of geometric motifs and some figurative elements in specific rooms, such as, for example, the image of a dog on a chain in the vestibule of a house. During the Imperial age a major development in mosaics led to a rich, geometric and figurative repertoire. In this period it became a widespread custom to cover fountains, nymphaeums and even the vaults of thermal baths with polychrome mosaics bordered with shells.
With the influx of marble from the Orient and Africa and with the opening of the quarries of Luni (Carrara) the use of marble floors became widespread (opus sectile) but, due to the systematic recycling of this precious material after the eruption of Vesuvius, few examples remain in Pompeii.

Furniture
In the houses of Pompeii, as in all Roman houses, there was usually little furniture, since interior architecture sometimes included built-in furniture such as cupboards, beds and tables. This made it possible to appreciate the pictorial decorations of the rooms integrally. We have a sufficiently complete knowledge of the furniture present in the houses thanks to that found in Pompeii and above all in Herculaneum.
Beds, both those used to sleep in (lectus cubicularis) and to recline on during meals (lectus tricliniaris), were often sumptuous pieces of furniture. The bedchamber bed could be a simple podium of stonework on which a mattress and pillows were placed, or else made of wood with bronze or silver trimmings, sometimes richly embellished with bone, ivory or tortoise shell. It often had a headboard or headboard and footboard (fulcra) and the mattress base (tortus, culcita) was made of wooden cross pieces and strips of cloth or leather. The legs of the bed were frequently shaped like coils, with rounded reliefs or bellflowers; and they were joined on the long or short sides by a shaped, wooden cross piece. Rocking cradles for babies also existed.
There were usually three types of trinclinium couch and they could have a stonework or wooden structure as had the beds for sleeping in. Small round or rectangular tables (mensae) made of wood, bronze or marble were placed in front of the couches, on which crockery and cutlery for the banquets were set. Larger round or rectangular tables were used for the serving dishes. Marble tables (cartibula) often ornamented the atria or gardens.
Chairs were very important items of furniture and various types existed. The subsellium or scamnum consisting of a simple wooden or bronze bench, functioned as a foot rest or was used for climbing into bed; the sellae with or without a back rest had fixed or sometimes folding legs; the solium, a

Reproduction of the decorative stuccoes from the Stabian Baths in Pompeii

Mosaic floor from Herculaneum. Royal Palace, Portici

quadrangular seat with a high back was destined for the *paterfamilias*; and the *cathedra*, of Greek derivation, was a typically feminine chair, elegant and comfortable, complete with a long, arched back and soft cushions. The *cathedrae* were also the characteristic seats of schoolteachers or priests.

To keep their possessions in order the Romans not only had chests and shelves like the Greeks, but also proper cupboards (*armaria*), which could be found in the bedrooms, dining rooms and also the atria. Wood was used exclusively for these items whilst the hinges were made of bone and the handles of metal. In the atrium of the *domus* bolted chests (*arcae*) were placed, which held the family patrimony and valuable documents. These chests were decorated with protoma and bronze busts of mythical subjects. Two of these chests can be seen in the atrium of the House of the Vettii. Feminine objects especially were kept in *cistae*, usually made of bronze, some beautiful examples of which are preserved in Pompeii.

*Bronze heaters.
National Archaeological
Museum, Naples*

*A triclinium couch in a
19th century engraving*

Systems of closure and security in the home

Many houses on Via dell'Abbondanza still preserve traces of ancient doors, sometimes reconstructed thanks to the use of plaster casts (21). The door (*ianua*), often framed by pillars surmounted by capitals, generally opened towards the interior of the house. Doors were wooden with two or more folding panels decorated with prominent, bronze knobs and supplied with a lock (*claustrum*) in bronze, usually with an L-shaped keyhole. The key (*clavis*) terminated with teeth corresponding to the bolt of the lock. Even inside the house individual rooms had doors, as shown by the presence of thresholds, which often preserve their bronze hinges or the holes into which the doors fitted.

Security constituted one of the principal worries of house owners: they maintained that locks were insufficient and there were other sophisticated systems of defence. The House of Ephebus (I, 7, 11) has one of the most complex systems of closure: the two panels of the door were secured by a metal lock with a key and bolted on the inside by a horizontal bar fixed into holes carved into the door jambs. In addition, there was another oblique bar, which was leant against the door panel which opened first, fixed at one end into a small cavity carved out for this purpose in the floor.

The most ancient Pompeian houses rarely had windows opening outwards,

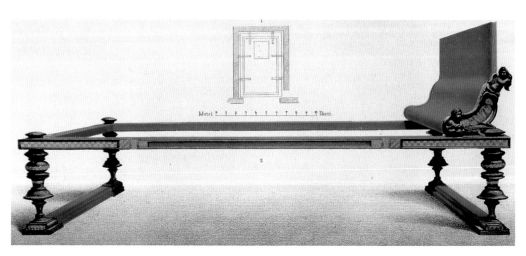

The metal grating in the atrium situated at the level of the compluvium prevented thieves from getting into houses. House I, 2, 28, Pompeii

The detail of this fresco in the Second Style, from Boscoreale, reproduces a panelled door and painting above the lintel. National Archaeological Museum, Naples

Bronze and lead kitchen utensils

terracotta gratings screened those without.

Even though the atrium was a precious source of lighting for the house, it also constituted a dangerous opening by which it was possible to violate the family's *privacy*. In fact it was easy to invade the intimacy of the home from adjacent houses, and Plautus makes one of his characters in a play say: "All my neighbours can see what goes on in my home because they look through my impluvium."

For this reason, iron rings have sometimes been found on the upper part of the columns supporting the roof of the atrium, which were used to stretch a blind (*velum*) across to protect the house from the sun and indiscreet eyes. Sometimes an iron grating was fixed at the height of the compluvium (such as in houses I, 2, 29, and IX, 2, 28) to protect the family from potential thieves who could have intruded through the roof.

Meals and banquets

The Roman house accomplished a wide range of duties and tasks: apart from being the family area, for rest and study, it was also the ideal framework for the social relationships of the owner, for which specific rooms were allocated. The best moment for celebrating and entertaining social acquaintances and friends was that of the banquet which generally began between the late afternoon and evening.

The Romans consumed three meals during the course of the day: morning breakfast, called *jentaculum*, consisting of a cup of milk or water, a biscuit dipped in wine, or a piece of bread and cheese; *prandium*, which was eaten around midday and consisted of a quick, cold meal often using up the leftovers from the previous day, or else of vegetables, eggs, fish and mushrooms; and finally dinner (*cena*), which constituted the main meal of the day and was conducted in a luxurious

and when they did they were shaped like embrasures, narrow and high off the ground. From the beginning of the 1st century AD the façades were animated by windows with glass panes, of which numerous fragments have been found in the excavations. The windowpanes varied in thickness from 1 centimetre to 4 millimetres, and were inserted into wooden or bronze frames, which opened turning vertically on two pivots in the middle of the frame at the top and bottom. The glass was rather opaque, and although it allowed light to pass through, one was not able to see the view outside clearly when the windows were closed. Not all of the houses had glass panes; wooden shutters or metal or

environment in the houses of the affluent. The ancient Romans, after having initially eaten around a fire, later took up the custom of eating in a reclined position in a special room: the triclinium, the use of which documents the advancing process of Hellenisation of the Roman culture. The same term *triclinium* is connected to the Greek word *kline* (bed) and the adoption of this room in the Roman house testifies to the new fashion of eating meals in a reclining position. The tricliniums were richly decorated rooms. In aristocratic houses there was more than one triclinium; there were winter tricliniums facing west to capture the last rays of the sun at sunset, and summer tricliniums, facing north to enjoy the coolness of the evening. Often summer tricliniums were in the open or situated alongside scenographic waterfalls and artificial streams (21).

The triclinium couches, often made of stonework, were arranged around three sides of a square or round table. Each couch had three places, so that nine people could eat in the same dining room. During the Imperial age couches with more than three places were also made and a *stibadium*, a type of curved couch. The three triclinium couches had different names; from right to left they were the *summus, medius* and *imus*. The guest of honour usually occupied the place called *locus consularis* at left end of the central couch, whilst the host sat on the right of the guest of honour. A guest would lie obliquely on the couch, facing the table, with his left elbow supported on a cushion. He would hold his plate in his left hand and, as forks were not used, he picked up food with the fingers of his right hand. Before serving the dishes, a slave would therefore cut the food into small pieces, which meant that knives were also not needed. Spoons were more widely used, which had different shapes according to their purpose. Very valuable china was used for the most important banquets, consisting of plates and vessels of decorated silver and glasses, bottles and goblets of glass or crystal.

The dinner was divided into three courses: the first course, called *gustatio*, consisted of an appetising dish designed to stimulate the appetite. This always

The garden of the House of the Vettii was decorated with small sculptures used as fountains

The arrangement of the guests' beds in the triclinium (Dosi-Schnell 1992)

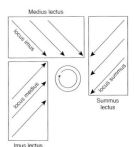

*Garden fresco from
Pompeii. National
Archaeological
Museum, Naples*

included eggs but vegetables and oysters could also be served. Then the main course followed, consisting of fish, meat and vegetables, and a second dish consisting usually of an elaborately prepared roast. The final course included desserts, and fresh and dried fruit, all of which was naturally washed down by wine, but usually in copious quantities towards the end of the meal to avoid compromising the taste of the dishes. During a banquet the guests wore light togas (*synthesis*), usually white in colour, which had to be changed if stained, and their heads were garlanded. A banquet could continue late into the night, thanks also to progress made in lighting techniques. A number of activities animated these evenings: concerts, recitals of verses, theatrical representations, and performances of dancing or jugglers. The *performances* by dwarves or foolish slaves, who entertained the guests with their witty remarks, were much appreciated. A further attraction was a draw offered by the host to his guests, consisting of gifts of perfumes, china, clothes, goblets, vases, food and birds.

Gardens

The most ancient Roman houses did not have real gardens, but a kitchen garden (*hortus*) instead, where vegetables and fruit were cultivated and sometimes oil and wine were produced for the needs of the household. Towards the end of the 2nd century BC, and particularly during the course of the 1st century BC, the *hortus* was surrounded by a portico (*peristylium*) and became progressively transformed into an artistically laid out garden. Alexandrian and Hellenistic culture influenced the old, naturalistic traditions of the Romans. Proper gardening techniques reached Rome, which brought the art of gardening to life (*ars topiaria* or *opus topiarium*). Large areas of the house were dedicated to the garden so that it became an essential and integral part of the house. During the Augustan age, with the construction of aqueducts, Pompeian gardens (*viridaria*) in urban houses became enriched by fountains, grottoes and nymphaeums, which reflected those typical elements of the great parks of the *otium* villas. Even large and small statues were adapted to spout jets of water, which then collected in marble basins to create complex water displays, such as those found in the House of the Vettii (11). Here there are some fourteen inter-connected fountains in the peristyle, as demonstrated by the ancient water system that is still clearly visible. The mild climate favoured life in the open air and in these green spaces we often find tricliniums, sometimes connected by water courses (*euripi*) as in the house of *Octavius Quartio* (21), or by gushing waterfalls issuing from a fake grotto, such as in the *praedia* of *Julia Felix* or in the house of Ephebus. Often the walls enclosing the gardens, the open-air tricliniums and the nymphaeums were decorated with paintings representing fruit trees, plants and flowers over which gracious birds flew, with the illusionary intention of transforming the entire environment into a sort of terrestrial, domestic paradise.

Ancient sources, pictorial representations, modern techniques of excavation and the analysis of seeds and pollen have allowed us to reconstruct in many cases the species cultivated in the *viridaria*. Evergreens, especially junipers, were generally planted in the flowerbeds, since their naturally regular foliage was suitable for the basic structure of the green architecture of the garden. Apart from flowers and small fruit trees that were naturally planted, medicinal and garland flowers such as myrtle and bay leaf were also cultivated, the latter being used to plait crowns.

Nymphaeum in the peristyle of the House of the Small Fountain in a 19th century engraving

Roads, traffic and public services

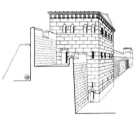

*The walls of Pompeii
(Maiuri 1943)*

The walls

The fortifications of Pompeii
The city of Pompeii is surrounded the length of its perimeter by walls (about 3.2 kilometres). The walls have been restored and reconstructed on numerous occasions, which, for the most part, are connected to the great military and historical events that affected the city. Seven gates open in the walls, and the existence of an eighth one (Porta Capua) has been hypothesised.
The oldest circle of wall, dating back to the 6th century BC, was made from blocks of lava and a soft, volcanic stone of a greyish-black colour. By the first half of the 5th century a new town wall had replaced the old one. The new fortification, perhaps due to Greek influence, was constructed by a double parallel ring of walls: to increase the capacity for resistance two rows of square blocks of Sarno limestone were arranged in horizontal rows.
Around the end of the 4th century BC the old fortifications were partially replaced by a new one, built on approximately the same line as the previous one, made of square blocks of Sarno limestone, alternately positioned by face or by side, with an embankment leaning against the inner wall. Probably the need to prepare the city against the incursions of the Carthaginians led by Hannibal (218-201 BC) was the main reason for the new restructuring of the fortifications. The single ring of walls with a rampart behind was replaced by a double ring with a new wall in tuff from

Nocera, built on the embankment, while the external ring was increased in height using new rows of blocks of the same material. Between the two rings of wall a communication patrol trench was created, accessible by means of special 'sloping' steps, still visible in part in the section of fortifications near the Porta Ercolano Gate.
The last intervention on the walls was undertaken around the period of the Social Wars (the end of the 2nd, beginning of the 1st century BC). Watch towers were added to the circuit of fortifications situated at more or less regular intervals, made of an unidentified material and covered in fake marble blocks of plaster as in the First style. The towers were of quadrangular form with battlements and had two access points: one from the base on the inside of the ring of walls and one from above from the patrol trench. They had two floors connected by ramps of steps that ran along the internal walls.
Embrasures opened at the height of each floor from which arrows and rock projectiles could be thrown. These new towers received a progressive numeration starting from Porta Stabia and following the perimeter of the wall in an anti-clockwise direction. We know this information from a rather unusual circumstance. During the Roman assault in the Social Wars, informative inscriptions in Oscan were painted (the so-called *eituns*) with the numbers of the various towers, which indicated to the soldiers running to help the

The Via di Mercurio in Pompeii

Pompeians the quickest routes to reach and occupy posts of combat on the walls. With the Roman conquest and the peace that followed, the walls progressively lost their defensive function. In certain sections, in particular the western and southern ones, they were built over by luxury edifices that exploited the dominant and panoramic position of the urban context.

Roads

The road network in Pompeii reflects the origin and development of the city. The streets of the original nucleus, which grew up around the Forum, were not all geometrically aligned. Subsequent districts amply demonstrate a more regular network of roads, characterised by main axial highways (*decumani*) which were crossed by minor streets (*cardini*) almost at rectangles, giving rise to isolated blocks (*insulae*) occupied by more than one house, or exceptionally by a single house or a public building.

The roads in Pompeii consist of a carriageway paved with large, polygonal

A gig for the transportation of people, found in the House of Menander, Pompeii

blocks of basalt, edged by a pavement generally higher than the road and reinforced with kerbs constituted by square blocks of lava, limestone or tuff, some of which preserve the marks of the Oscan stonecutters.

One can sometimes note holes on the edges of the pavements, probably used to hold the posts which either supported street stalls or sunblinds, or else, according to another hypothesis, were used to tie up transport animals.

To facilitate pedestrian crossing and to protect pedestrians' feet from rainwater or refuse water, which flowed down the carriageway, some ovoid-shaped stepping-stones were placed between the two pavements, which were also made from basalt, as was the road surface. Between one to four of these stepping stones were used according to the width of the road, and were generally placed where needed, in correspondence with the entrances to houses and public buildings, etc. There were also other stones placed vertically along the edge of the pavements, which functioned as kerbstones. Irregular stones that were located on the sides of or around the fountains had the same function, that is to protect the water pipes from carriage wheels.

Urban traffic

The streets of Pompeii were very lively. From the large number of shops and stores present we can visualise a city animated by the bustle of merchants, shopkeepers and customers.

Merchandise was frequently displayed on the pavements, and there were a lot of peddlers, idlers and beggars. Even teachers held their lessons in the open air on the streets or under the shelter of porches or awnings.

A lively picture of daily life is shown to us in a series of frescoes found in the *Praedia* of *Julia Felix* and now preserved in the National Museum of Naples. Against the background of the colonnades of a portico (probably that of the Forum in Pompeii), these frescoes represent traders of cloth, shoes, saucepans and metal tools, and even a teacher whipping a student in the presence of a group of pupils seated at their desks.

One sign of the intensity of the traffic is shown by the deep furrows left by carriage wheels on the carriageways – carriages being the main means of transport in Pompeii. These furrows are most prominent where the circulation of traffic was busiest, and probably constituted a sort of guide for the carriage wheels, which would have had approximately the same inter-axial distance. Ancient sources mention varies types of vehicle in circulation: ceremonial carriages (*tensa, pilentum*), travel vehicles (*carpentum, cisium, carruca, rheda*) and others for carrying goods (*plaustrum, carrus*). The only preserved Roman vehicle for the transportation of passengers in existence comes from Pompeii: the iron structure has been completely salvaged and the wooden part has been restored. It was found in the House of Menander (I, 10, 4) and is a gig with two high wheels, which could easily pass over the pedestrian crossings. Suitable for rapid travel, it was pulled by a horse and could carry two people. This was probably the most widely used type of carriage for urban transport. Vehicles

for transporting goods were much more solid, they had two full wheels on which a wooden top with side panels rested and it was pulled by mules or oxen. An example of this type of vehicle comes from Villa Regina in Boscoreale, while a carriage with four wheels whose circumference reaches 1.17 metres was found in Stabiae.

The roads in Pompeii are of different widths: Via dell'Abbondanza, the *decumanus maximus* (the main road), is 8.47/8.53 metres wide, while Via Stabiana, the most important of the minor roads is between 7.15 and 7.47 metres wide; but there were also much narrower roads which raised the problem of traffic regulation. Although a carriage could pass in practically all the streets of the city, two-way circulation of traffic was impossible. It would seem that two-way circulation was excluded because, in many cases, it was impossible for the driver to see if another carriage coming from the opposite direction was turning into the same street. If two carriages had met with such a difficulty, one of the two would have had to reverse and the presence of pedestrian stepping-stones would have further complicated the situation.

In all probability traffic in the narrow streets would not have circulated freely, but would have been regulated by a one-way system. In addition, some streets were completely closed to traffic, such as the Forum square, where access was barred by huge rectangular stones fixed solidly into the ground, or the section to

Wayfarer and witch, fresco from the House of the Dioscuri, Pompeii. National Archaeological Museum, Naples

the west of Via dell'Abbondanza – inaccessible due to the difference in levels and because of barriers placed at the edges of the converging side streets – or Via di Mercurio.

There were also parking areas for vehicles in the vicinity of the gates. Mule-drivers and coachmen (*muliones*) stopped for example in the vicinity of Porta Stabiana, whilst gigs (*cisarii*) were parked in the vicinity of Porta Ercolano (CIL, X, 1064). Their duties were to transport passengers or goods between the countryside and the city; the *muliones* also looked after animals used for the postal service.

Shops, 'bars', taverns, and workshops animated the main streets of Pompeii; in fact the highest concentration of these public enterprises was found alongside the principal streets. Even though there is not a neat division between rich and poor districts in Pompeii, and often a large *domus* was situated next to a modest house, it is generally evident that those who could afford to sought to occupy housing in areas with less traffic. This is the case of the luxury residences along Via di Mercurio, where traffic was prohibited. Those who could not afford to would have shared the experience of Martialis, who complained that at night the traffic shook the *insulae* (IV, 64, 20); or Jovenal, who complained in a famous satire: "But is there a house for rent in Rome which allows one to sleep? It is only possible to sleep with a small fortune. The carriages which go up and down into the depths of the alleyways, and the herds of animals which stop and make a din which would wake Drusus or a sea lion, are to blame for this ailment." (III, 234-248: Drusus was famous for sleeping deeply and the sea lion was considered a very sleepy animal).

Road Maintenance

The city roads were public property. Nevertheless, their maintenance and cleaning was provided by the collaboration of the owners of the houses fronting the road, in proportion to the length and width of each house (*Tabula Heraclensis*, 20; 32; 50). This collaboration was exclusively financial, not direct. The maintenance work was overseen by local magistrates (*aediles and curatores viarium*) within a system of tender. Although the onus was on householders, the road and pavement outside their homes were still public spaces, and consequently the doors of the houses were hinged to open inwards, towards the atrium, rather than outwards, so as not to encroach on public property.

Street wolves

Walking in the crowded streets of Pompeii was a complicated affair, not only because of the traffic. Sometimes those out for a walk or simply going from one place to another were molested for sexual reasons. In fact, even from that time, the streets were frequented by men following young women, whispering compliments and making proposals – more or less *osées* – (and which were accepted favourably or not): as we would say today, "street wolves". Such was the frequency of this type of behaviour, that the city praetor was obliged to issue an edict against anyone molesting the *matresfamilias* (that is honest women) in the streets, and even (given that the Romans were not averse to encounters with good-looking men) the young *praetextati*, that is the youths who wore a white tunic with a purple border (*praetexta*) reserved for those too young for political capacity.

The edict also specified which particular acts of molestation were punishable: the *adsectatio*, which consisted of following the object of courtship in silence but with insistence; the *appelatio*, which consisted of uttering flattery and persuasive comments (*blanda oratio*) to the woman or youth, and finally the *comitum abductio*, that is the removal of the guardian escort who accompanied young females and *pratextati*.

Although the edict referred particularly to the city of Rome, the nature of sexual morality of the Romans and Pompeians (revealed among other things by evidence from graffiti) undoubtedly justifies our belief that this type of behaviour was certainly not uncommon.

Road names and the current division of the urban area

The denomination of the roads in Pompeii is modern. They derive from the most important houses on the streets (Vicolo dei Vettii), or from a representation of a fountain (Via dell'Abbondanza), or from an archaeological discovery (Vicolo dei Cinque Scheletri) or from a visit by a famous person (Via della Regina). In the majority of cases we ignore the original names of the streets, since, we do not know, except in rare circumstances, the name of the family or owner who lived in a particular house.

The division of the urban area of Pompeii into *Regiones* (districts) and *Insulae* (blocks) was made by the archaeologist Giuseppe Fiorelli in 1858, who also assigned a number to each house in Pompeii in order to provide a denomination and an exact location. Probably in Pompeii, as in Rome, only some of the most important streets were named. Civic house numbers did not exist and so orienting oneself or searching for someone was based on reference to public buildings in the immediate vicinity, or on the most frequent type of shop in a certain street (the antecedents of the various streets of the Shoemakers, Goldsmiths etc.)

Public and private lighting

For lighting, the Romans used a variety of lamps in terracotta, bronze, iron, glass or even gold. The most common type of lamp consisted of a container in which oil was burnt, with a neck from which the wick emerged for the light, a hole for the fuel and a handle (*ansa*) for carrying the lamp. This simple form could have a number of variations, beginning with that with two necks (*bilicini* lamps) or more (*policini* lamps) to provide better illumination. Especially during the Imperial age the upper part of the oil lamp (disk) was decorated with a single figure or more detailed scenes. The most recurrent decorative themes included divinities (Mercury, Diana, Jupiter, cupids etc.), gladiatorial contests, horse races, erotic scenes, theatrical masks, animals, plants and other objects. During the 1st century AD, lamps were made in the shape of gladiator helmets, Negroid heads, animal heads and shod sandals, to satisfy the tastes of clients searching for original objects.

Lamps were complimented by supports, constituted by branched candlesticks, candlesticks and bases, of which a number of examples are preserved in Pompeii. Candlesticks were usually bronze, consisting of a long stem on a base formed by three, wild animal hooves and a circular crown on which the light was placed. Due to their value, these objects became important elements of domestic furnishing, in particular in the dining room during banquets, especially as they allowed more diffused lighting in the room. There were also very precious supports, such as the so-called 'torchers', consisting of real statues, usually bronze, representing young people holding vases in their hands on which the light was placed. A particularly beautiful statue was found in the house of Fabius Rufus, another in Via dell'Abbondanza, and an Apollo from the house of Julius Polybius.

Lamps were not limited to private and domestic use: they were also utilised in temples, thermal baths, theatres and amphitheatres during evening

Terracotta lamp. National Archaeological Museum, Naples

performances. Lamps were also used for shop lighting. There is a *bilicine* lamp from a thermopolium in Via dell'Abbondanza which is joined in the middle by fine chains to the figure of a pigmy with a huge phallus, which also has the function of bringing good fortune.

Texts of ancient authors recount that the darkness of the streets was one of the main causes of aggression and accidents. During all journeys undertaken at night, it was sensible to send a slave on ahead with a torch or a lantern. Svetonius (*Vita Aug.*, 29) recounts that even travelling carriages were preceded by a slave with a torch.

Water supply

Originally the problem of water supply was solved by the Pompeians using tanks located in the gardens and the atria of the houses, fed by rainwater which flowed from the roof (impluvium) into a pool below (compluvium), and from there into the tank. Water was collected from the tank by means of a well situated in the atrium or peristyle, which had a cylindrical stone or terracotta well curb, often decorated, around the opening. Even public buildings used cisterns, especially the thermal baths, without which they could not function. Additional wells for the irrigation of the fields and other needs

were provided by digging through the seam of lava and tuff on which the city was built, as far as the water-bearing stratum.

During the Augustan age the supply of water improved considerably with the construction of an aqueduct fed by the springs of Acquaro, near Serino. From here the aqueduct passed through various localities, reaching Nola and Pompeii, whilst another branch reached Naples. The Pompeian branch reached the city at its highest point, near Porta Vesuvio, where a huge tank, called *castellum acquae*, collected the water and redistributed it into three conduits that constituted the main branches of the urban water supply. It has been hypothesised that the three-way partition of the Pompeian *castellum acquae* corresponds to that indicated by Vitruvius (VIII, 6), who suggested that the *castellum acquae* should be divided into three tanks for the main consumers of the city: private housing, the thermal baths, fountains and water displays. The three water mains leaving the *castellum acquae* of Pompeii supplied minor distributors displaced along the main route and also functioned to reduce the water pressure in the pipelines. These structures, in the form of pillars, had a vertical groove along which the canalised water was first forced upwards to reach a lead tank (*castellum*

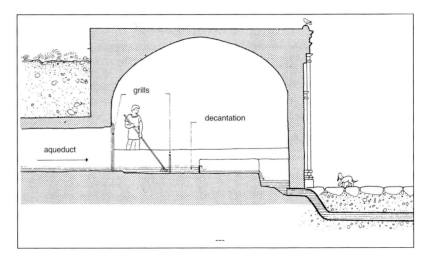

Cross-section of the castellum acquae, the large tank which collected water and redistributed it throughout the city by means of three canals (Adam 1989)

plumbeum) placed at the top, and then descended, in order to regulate the flow and pressure. The conduits for the adduction of water were made of lead, the pipes (*fistulae*), still visible at various places in Pompeii, were elliptical in cross section and of different sizes and were occasionally marked with a monogram. There were also terracotta pipes, used especially for the discharge of waste; numerous examples of which can be seen in the walls of the houses for the drainage of water from the upper floors.

The water mains in Pompeii were damaged in the earthquake of '62, but were very probably repaired quickly; otherwise it is impossible to explain the construction of the new thermal baths, named the Central Baths, undertaken just after the earthquake. At the time of the eruption in 79 it appears that the urban water mains system was being rebuilt– probably necessitated by the damage caused by the earthquake that preceded the catastrophic eruption –and the lead pipelines were being embedded at a certain depth to avoid easy damage.

Public fountains

The largest quantity of water was reserved for public fountains, where the water flowed day and night (while other consumers had taps to regulate the flow

of water), and which were also utilised to clean the streets. To meet the needs of the population, the fountains were placed at a distance from each other, which varied from between 70 and 80 metres, so that citizens could always count on a supply of water near their homes. About forty fountains have been discovered in Pompeii and they vary little in form; they have a rectangular basin made of four stone slabs usually of lava, joined by iron cramps. Water is transported by a lead pipe and gushes out of a decorative spout.

The drainage system

With the exception of the area of the Forum, Pompeii had no drainage network and so excess or dirty water ran directly onto the streets. However, the streets were built on an incline and the water flowed out of the city following the natural slope of the highways to join special, open outlets at the foot of the city walls. To obviate the inconvenience of this constant presence of water along the kerbs of the streets, which quite naturally created difficulties for citizens, the stepping stones mentioned previously – large square slabs of lava – were placed across the streets to enable pedestrians to cross without getting their feet wet.

Latrines

The term *latrina* or *lavatrina* derives
from the Latin verb *lavare*, and in fact in
ancient times the *latrina* was a place to
wash oneself. When the first public
baths were built and when private baths
were installed in the houses of the
wealthiest, the *latrina* remained only as a
sanitary installation.

Latrines were installed in many houses
in Pompeii. Sometimes they were also
found on the upper floors and they
shared the same piping as drainage
water. However, public latrines existed
(*foricae*): at least five have been
identified in Pompeii. Naturally they
were situated in well-frequented
districts: one in the Forum, another
three close to the Suburban Baths, the
Central Thermal Baths and the Stabian
Baths respectively, and another near the
Palaestra. Another two latrines were
annexed to Baths of Sarno and the
praedia of Julia Felix, but it is not
possible to ascertain whether they were
public services or reserved for a select

clientele who frequented these
establishments. The latrine of the Forum
(VII, 7, 28), not in use at the time of the
eruption of 79, was screened from the
street by an entrance hall and could
accommodate up to twenty people.
The working of these latrines was almost
identical. A drain ran along three sides
of the room in which water flowed
continuously. There were stonework
supports above the drains in which
stone or marble seats were set.
The discharge water under these seats was
conveyed to the nearest sewer or cess-
pit. The sanitary fittings were completed
by a washstand or small basin in which
water ran continuously. In the course of
time some latrines even came to assume
the form of a monument and they could
be richly decorated. The latrines
annexed to the thermal baths in Pompeii
preserve a certain aesthetic dignity: in
the latrine of the Suburban Baths, for
example, is the representation of an
erect Fortune near a small altar with a
helm in her hands and a globe at her
feet. A similar type of representation is

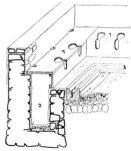

*One of the numerous
public fountains at the
crossroads of the city,
in a 19th century
etching*

*Structure of a Roman
latrine:*
1. *Wooden seat*
2. *Sewer*
3. *Pipe for running
   water*

Via dell'Abbondanza, the main road in Pompeii. One of the numerous public fountains of the city is in the foreground

testified in another four *toilettes* in Pompeii: probably the image was held to bode well and protect the latrine from the evil eye. In one of these paintings with Fortune, which comes from tavern IX, 7, 22 and is currently held at the National Museum of Naples (inv. N. 112285), there is the inscription *Cacator cave malum* above a man in the act of defecating, and which has been interpreted as a warning to servants to only use the latrines to satisfy certain physiological needs. Pompeii bears witness to the practice of writing in charcoal or graphite on the walls of toilets, and was very widespread amongst the Romans, as even Martialis noted (XII, 61).

Evidently such places have always inspired their users to leave written evidence – often vulgar– of their presence.

Relaxation and entertainment

It was current opinion among moralists of the Roman age that their fellow-citizens were only interested in wine, gambling, fun and shows. In fact, there were numerous occasions for festivals and shows especially during the Imperial age: religious holidays, military victories, the inauguration of temples and the anniversaries of the emperors. The people rushed enthusiastically to watch the public games, which became a powerful means of popular consent. In Pompeii, as in all Romanised cities, the public games (*gladia, ludi*) were not only important occasions for recreation but also for political life. Magistrates and those aspiring to political careers vied with each other to offer the most extravagant and spectacular entertainment to their fellow-citizens. Various types of *ludi* existed: those that were held in the Arena (*ludi circenses*), consisting principally of chariot racing; theatrical representations (*ludi scaenici*) and other amphitheatre performances (*munera*). The most popular entertainment for the crowds were gladiatorial contests held initially in the Forum, but which, from the age of Caesar, took place in specially constructed amphitheatres. The amphitheatre of Pompeii, in particular, was among the oldest of those known to us (22).

Gladiatorial contests

For the most part gladiators were either prisoners of war or those condemned to death. On occasion, men condemned to forced labour were sent into combat, who, if victorious could obtain their freedom, and also slaves, who were hired out by their own masters. Lastly, gladiators might also be free men, who for necessity, or desire for fame and fortune, voluntarily contracted themselves to a *lanista*. This was a character of dubious reputation who managed and maintained the gladiatorial *familia*: he was responsible for organising and directing the specialised schools in which the gladiators were trained for combat (the most famous being that of Capua, where the revolt of Spartacus erupted), and also for organising the contests. All those who intended to offer gladiatorial contests (*munera*) to the people for special occasions or holidays, and even magistrates, who were obliged to offer shows during their year in office, had to apply to the *lanista*.

During the Republican age gladiators wore clothing which was similar to that of a soldier's, but from the age of Augustus onwards gladiators were divided into proper classes on the basis of the type of arms they carried and on the type of combat they engaged in: the *retiarius*, was armed with a trident and a net, with which he tried to immobilise his opponent; the *oplomaco* took his name from the large shield used to protect him; the *dimachaerus* fought with two knives; the *sagittarius* used a bow and arrows as arms; the *murmillo* was armed with a sword and a lance and used a rectangular shield for protection, and the *essedarius* fought from a chariot of war.

Gladiator helmet with scenes from the fall of Troy, from Pompeii. National Archaeological Museum, Naples

Chariot race, fresco from the House of the Quadriga, Pompeii. National Archaeological Museum, Naples

The gladiators' lives were very hard; they lived in barracks and were subjected to constant training. A gladiators' neighbourhood even existed in Pompeii, probably in that district which was appropriately called "The Gladiators' Barracks" (V, 5, 3) where numerous graffiti were found on the twenty-four columns of the peristyle, left by the gladiators who had lived there. Following the earthquake of 62 the 'Barracks' were probably no longer practicable and the gladiators were accommodated in the large quadriporticus annexed to the theatre. There were many occasions during combat in which a gladiator could lose his life. If he were defeated but did not die, his fate depended on the mood of the public. If the spectators shouted '*missum*' (free) his life was saved, if they gave him the thumbs down signal (*pollice verso*), he was killed. Nevertheless, particularly brave gladiators not only earned large sums of money, but also became real idols of the crowds. In this regard, Pompeian graffiti are particularly illuminating: a certain Oceanus, for example, after having won thirteen contests, became the city mascot (CIL IV, 8055 a); the Tracean Celadus was highly desired by young

women (*Suspirium puellarum Celadus thraex*, CIL IV, 4379); and another graffito announced that the retiarius Crescens "is the whores' doctor" (*Crescens retarius puparum nocturnarum…medicus*, CIL IV, 4353). If we are prepared to believe Jovenal (*Sat.*, IV 103ss), noble ladies had a weakness for gladiators, who were considered the more virile the more they were disfigured in combat. There are also those who maintain that the bejewelled body of a noble lady, a victim of the eruption, found in the gladiators' barracks is proof of an adventurous and fatal encounter (given the outcome)

between a Pompeian lady and a passing champion.

However exciting, gladiatorial contests were not the most spectacular forms of entertainment, not even when, on the same day, as many as thirty fighting pairs of gladiators – and their substitutes (*supposticii*) – took part in the games ordered by Gnaeus Alleius Nigidius Maius (CIL, IV, 7991).

In fact, the most spectacular games were the *venationes*, in which hunters (*venatores*) fought against wild animals. During the first show of this type offered to the Romans in 186 BC, lions and panthers were imported from

19th century reconstruction of the performance of a wild animal hunt in the Amphitheatre of Pompeii

Reconstruction of a gladiatorial contest held in Nola. Graffiti on tomb no. 19 of the Necropolis of Porta Nocera in Pompeii

*Mosaic from the
House of the Tragic
Poet showing actors
preparing for
the performance
of a satirical drama.
On the right-hand side
and on the ground
are some masks worn
by the actors on stage.
National Archaeological
Museum, Naples*

Ethiopia. Then, in time, panthers, bears, elephants, rhinoceroses, deer, monkeys, giraffes and every other type of foreign animal were brought in from the conquered territories. The massacre of the animals provoked by these shows was horrifying: Pompaeus had five hundred lions killed in five days, Caesar sacrificed four hundred in one show only, and during the government of Augustus, during the course of twenty-six *venationes* three thousand five hundred African animals were killed. These figures of course have no

relationship to those in Pompeii which were certainly more modest, but this does not mean that shows of this kind were not held in the Campanian city, such as the one, for example, during which a certain Felix fought against bears (*V Kalendis Septembris Felix ad ursos pugnabit*, CIL IV, 1989). Generally, amphitheatre shows consisted of one gladiatorial contest and one *venatio* (animal hunt), as confirmed by the *edicta munerum*, that is, the announcements of the shows painted on the walls of Pompeii.

Preparation for such events, involved the setting up of various facilities to make the time spent in the amphitheatre, which was often long, more comfortable for the public. A large tarpaulin was erected to protect the spectators from the sun and rain (*velarium*), as shown in a painting representing the amphitheatre of Pompeii during the riot between the Pompeians and Nocerines. To relieve the spectators of the heat and unpleasant smells produced by the animals, *sparsiones* were also provided, which consisted of fine, perfumed jets of water which were sprayed from conduits under the arena (Seneca, *Nat. Quaest.*, II 9,1). These types of conduits have not been found in the amphitheatre of Pompeii, but a few announcements for these shows seem to refer to these types of facilities.

The enthusiasm of the Pompeians for these games was matched by their unruliness. Tacitus recounts (*Annales* XIV, 17) that, in 59 AD during a gladiatorial contest organised by Livineius Regolus on the initiative of the Senate, a serious episode of urban warfare broke out between the local *ultras* and those of the neighbouring city of *Nuceria* (Nocera).

"At the beginning" – writes Tacitus – "as often happens in provincial cities, the spectators derided each other by exchanging insults and vulgarities; then passed to throwing stones and finally to the use of arms. The Pompeian supporters, being more numerous given that the game was held at home, came off the better. Many Noceran supporters were carried home badly injured and many grieved the death of a son or father". Because of the severity of the episode the amphitheatre of Pompeii was banned from holding games for the next ten years. The organisers and those who led the rioting were sentenced to exile. The parallels between these 'hooligans' of the ancient world and the behaviour which frequently characterises certain contemporary sporting events highlight a specific social phenomenon: the concept of sport typical of ancient Greek society, founded on individual prowess, was replaced in Rome by a popular, collective and violent management of sport which for better or worse is replicated in the present day.

Theatrical performances

The theatre was one of the highest cultural expressions of the Greek and Roman civilizations. Tragedy and above all comedy were the main genres of the Roman theatre, predominantly influenced by Greek theatre. Greek tragedy and comedy continued to be performed for many centuries, but there were also performances produced in Italy by playwrights such as Nevius, Plautus, Ennius, Terentius and Seneca. Alongside early and traditional forms of theatre new genres and those of local derivation gradually appeared. Amongst these was the *fabula atellana*, a type of popular farce of Oscan origin which depicted situations of crude and spicy realism, often bordering on the obscene, and which attracted a large following in Pompeii too. In these farces humble characters were reproduced, some of whom were represented by masks, with fixed roles such as *Pappus*, the old fool, *Maccus*, the glutton and *Dossenus*, the crafty one, who pre-date Harlequin and Punch in the Comedy of Arts. Another performance of popular and farcical origin was mime, which was very successful, especially from the beginning of the age of Caesar. Characterised by short, light and amusing plots, and by dialogue rich in obscene double meanings, mime adapted well to the taste of the Roman people, but not only them. Sulla was also a noted mime enthusiast and he had an actor friend who specialised in feminine roles (Plutarch, *Sull.*, 36,2). Pantomime followed on from mime, in which the

Musicians performing in the street. Detail of a mosaic from Pompeii signed by Dioskourides. National Archaeological Museum, Naples

actors, accompanied by a chorus and musicians, played characters and interpreted mythological themes using only mime, without help from words. In general, actors performed on stage wearing wigs and different coloured clothes. The colours were chosen on purpose: each one had a conventional value that allowed immediate recognition of the characters (their social status and age) even from a distance. The actors' faces were hidden by masks (*persona*) with a funnel-shaped opening for the mouth that amplified speech. Even though none of these masks have been preserved, we know that they were made from light wood or plaster-soaked cloth, complete with hair and beards made from hide or other materials. We know what they looked like from numerous reproductions in marble and terracotta, from paintings and mosaics and from the descriptions given us by the grammarian Julius Pollux, in his work *Onomastikon* (IV, 133-154). Different types of masks were utilised for tragedy and comedy: the tragic mask was generally characterised by a hairstyle lifted high off the forehead (*onkos*); the comic one by a rolled up hairstyle with or without curls; old people and slaves were generally bald whilst young people were curly-haired and blond. Feminine masks existed too with straight, frizzy or curly hair, even though they were worn by male actors. Actors of mime were dressed in striking clothes and a cloak (*ricinium*) and performed barefoot and without masks because their facial expressions helped their acting (real mime). In mime feminine roles were acted for the first time by women, who naturally earned spurious reputations. In fact they often undressed on stage, or consented to the *nudatio mimarum*, a type of strip–tease, which the spectators demanded loudly. Actors, especially pantomime actors, enjoyed great popularity with the public. We know the names of some actors who worked both in Pompeii and in Rome, such as the pantomime artists *Theorus* and *Pierus*, or the much–acclaimed Pilad. A bronze portrait has also been found of another famous actor, Norbanus Sorex, in the Temple of Isis. Certain Pompeian graffiti applaud famous actors like Paris, probably the same one who Nero had killed, who considered him an awe-inspiring rival (Svetonius, *Nero*, 54); whilst another actor, *C. Ummidius Actius Anicetus* was acclaimed by his *fans* who called themselves *Actiani Anicetiani* after the name of their mascot. For a long time theatrical performances were held on temporary stages erected in squares and in front of temples. Proper theatres in stonework were built progressively throughout the whole of Italy, inspired by the Greek theatres. From the 2nd century BC the city of Pompeii had a stonework theatre: the Large Theatre, built near the southern edge of the city (monument 15). We imagine that theatrical events were frequent in Pompeii, since apart from the Large Theatre, the Odeion was also built as a music hall (monument 16).

The lively interest in and familiarity with the theatre, also appears through the work of decorators and of their Pompeian commissioners in wall paintings depicting scenes from the tragedies, and through the vast number of masks created in marble, in paintings and in mosaics, which decorate many houses in the city.

Athletic games

Especially from the beginning of the 1st century BC, athletic games on the model of the Olympic Games (*certamina graeca*) were also organised in ancient Rome. These games found favour with Augustus who then instigated the *Sebastà* in Naples, the famous athletic games held in honour of the Emperor every four years. Nero, also a staunch admirer of Greek customs, organised

the *Neronia* in Rome, which included horse races, musicals and gymnastic events (Svetonius, *Nero*, 12).
Athletic disciplines included a track race (the unit of measurement being equal to 600 feet or about 180 metres), a race in armour, a relay, a torch race, the long jump, throwing the javelin and the discus, and horse races. Heavy athletics consisted of wrestling, boxing and the pancratium. All types of holds were permitted in wrestling including the leg lock, and the winner was he who managed to throw his opponent down three times. In boxing the contestants fought with gloves tightly laced with strips of leather that reached from the middle forearm to the hands, leaving the tips of the fingers free. In the Roman age boxing gloves (*caesti*) were reinforced with metal, which made the contests crueller. There were no rest intervals allowed in boxing, one fought until one's opponent was knocked out or withdrew. The pancratium was a contest in which everything was permitted: kicking, boxing, twisting of the joints, breaking of bones and attempts at strangulation, with the exception of biting and scratching. We know that even women participated in certain athletic games: some young girls took part in the track racing in Rome (Suet., *Dom.*, 4) and some magistrates' daughters attempted the same race in the *Sebastà* in Naples. The practice of athletics was not limited to professional competitors. The passion for sport involved everyone and places designated for gymnastics were present in every Roman city, as in Pompeii. The Emperor Augustus in particular promoted physical activity amongst the young by creating associations (*collegia*) where, together with the body, the conscience of virtue (*virtus*) and political loyalty were shaped in the children of bourgeois citizens. Documentation on one of these youth associations (*Iuventus*

Pompeiana) comes from Pompeii where boys and girls between the ages of eleven and seventeen met to exercise and organise games (*ludus iuvenum* or *iuvenalia*) in honour of the goddess *Iuventus*, patroness of youth. During these festivals the young people took part in various performances among which the most famous was the so-called *lusus Troiae*, consisting of a series of elaborate evolutions, one of which was represented by a snake-like movement (S shaped) of the group. One particular Pompeian inscription (CIL IV, 1595) demonstrates the lively interest provoked by this exercise.
The construction of the Large Palaestra in Pompeii for sports training of the young bears witness to the impetus given by the Emperor Augustus to sporting activities (monument 23). Physical exercise was also cultivated by the users of the gymnasiums that were annexed to the thermal baths, because they believed that it complemented the beneficial effects of the waters.

Thermal baths

Thermal baths constitute one of the most characteristic achievements of Roman architecture. Despite having Greek baths as a point of reference, Roman baths developed in an original form and acquired widespread popularity in the course of time, becoming an authentic phenomenon of custom, the expression of a particular concept of life and a compulsory daily need. Frequenting the baths became an established daily routine: if not the most important it was certainly the most pleasurable. That which contributed to making the baths one of the favourite places to spend one's free time was the opportunity to satisfy not only the well-being of the body but also of the spirit. In fact, in the course of time, large thermal complexes added porticos, gardens, nymphaeums, living and rest rooms, musical auditoriums, and

libraries to the areas already designated for bathing. One went to the baths not only to practise physical exercises and fortify oneself with the waters and complementary therapeutic practices (massage, rubbing and oiling the body) but also to stroll, meet people, conduct business and to give and receive invitations.
Despite the variety of thermal establishments, the rigid succession of the various phases of bathing determined a canonical plan for the layout of the baths, which in the Pompeian examples present a more or less identical succession of rooms along a longitudinal axis. After passing through the entrance hall there was a waiting room and changing room (*apodyterium*), furnished with marble or bronze benches and with wooden or stonework shelves along the walls where bathers put their clothes and personal possessions. Valuables were left in the custody of *capsarii*, the servants of the baths, who looked after personal property for payment. In fact, robbery in the baths was common, necessitating careful and constant surveillance. The next room was the *frigidarium*, an area with a pool or a bath of cold water located in the same room or in an adjacent open-air one. Then the *tepidarium* followed, a passageway between the *frigidarium* and the *calidarium*, created to avoid too rapid temperature changes. Annexed to the *tepidarium* was usually the *laconicum*, a circular area used for the dry heat bath (sauna). Following this was the *calidarium*, a room used for the hot bath. In the Pompeian examples these rooms generally had a rectangular plan with an apse on one of the short sides. In the apse we find the *labrum*, a marble basin used for cold-water ablutions intended to lower the body temperature to increase tolerance to the heat inside the *calidarium*.
On the opposite side to the apse was the

The calidarium of the Forum Baths. On one side is the pool for the hot bath, on the other the basin for cold water to cool the bathers

A *thermopolium* in Pompeii. Food and hot drinks were served on these premises. The large jars (*dolia*) containing the snacks were encased in the counters

alveus, a rectangular pool for the hot bath. The *alveus* was constructed in stonework and lined with marble and it had one or more steps along the internal walls to allow the bathers to sit in the hot water. The heating system was initially provided by braziers. At the beginning of the 1st century BC, heating techniques were revolutionised, probably due to the invention of a rich Campanian businessman, Sergio Orata, and this improved the sanitary and hygienic conditions of the baths. The new technique, invented for oyster breeding, consisted in the circulation of hot air through spaces located in the walls and floors. The hot air came from water heated in stoves in areas (*preafurnium*) generally situated at the back of the *calidarium*. The floor interstices (*hypocaustum*) were made with rows of brick pillars (*pilae*) generally between 70 and 90 centimetres in height. The flooring of the room, often made of marble tiles, as these provided good heat conductors, was placed over this board of pillars

(*suspensurae*). The wall interstices (*concameratio*) were created by placing large tiles on the walls fitted with breast-shaped protuberances at their four corners (*tegulae mammate*) to distance them from the walls, or by using terracotta pipes (*tubuli*). This system was capable of ensuring temperatures of over 30° (and even up to 60°) and of maintaining these high temperatures constantly.

Many thermal baths housed a gymnasium with a portico, where various sporting activities took place, such as wrestling, and games with a ball and with a hoop.

Pompeii had at least three thermal baths, and a fourth, the Central Baths, were under construction at the time of the eruption of 79. The oldest were the Stabian Baths, the first installation dating to the 4th century BC, while the Forum Baths probably date to the period of the founding of the Sullan colony. More recent (the first decade of the 1st century AD) and more in keeping with dictates of fashion were

the Suburban Baths, built close to the walls immediately outside Porta Marina. These baths, in contrast to the other two, were not divided into male and female sections. For a long time it was hypothesised that baths with only one section, which became common in the 1st century AD, had different opening hours: women attending in the morning and men in the afternoon. In reality, at least for the 1st century, there is no proof of alternate use, while numerous literary references exist testifying to the communal practice of bathing. In practice, whilst admitting that regulations regarding bathing rotas existed, these were neither applied nor respected, since during the course of time a series of imperial constitutions were released which prohibited promiscuous bathing. The practice of communal bathing scandalised many Roman writers, especially as, according to certain sources, men and women bathed naked. ("When I praise your face, Galla, and I admire your legs and

This painting on marble from Herculaneum represents the myth of Niobes children: the goddess Phoebe tries to reconcile Niobes and the goddess Leto, while in the foreground two Niobes' daughters play with astragals, a game similar to dice. National Archaeological Museum, Naples

hands, you always say "you surely prefer me naked". But then you refuse to bathe with me. Perhaps I please you less in the nude?" Martialis, III, 51).

Inns and taverns

We have already seen how important shops, wine bars and inns were in the commercial life of the city, but they were also important for social life and leisure time. There were a considerable number of these establishments in Pompeii. They were uniformly distributed throughout the city, although there is an increased concentration in *Regiones I* and *II*, in proximity to the Amphitheatre – which attracted a large number of people from the city and its surroundings – and to the access Gates to the city, which provided the first refreshments to arriving travellers. Some of these establishments were furnished with only a stone counter, which encased the *dolia* which contained wine, and where customers were served standing; others had an inside room, where one could sit down, and even others had tricliniums for their more refined clientele.
Not only did one eat in these establishments, but one also passed the time in various occupations. One of the most dangerous attractions was gambling, prohibited by law, alongside betting. Amongst the most widespread games of chance were astragals and dice. Astragals were made from certain bones from the feet of sheep. Usually four or five were used to play and conventional values were attributed to each face, which had different configurations. Astragals had to be thrown up in the air and caught on the back of the hand; a player who dropped any had to pick them up without dropping any of those already caught. Players gained different points according to the combination of the various faces obtained by a throw. The best points were for "the throw of Venus", in which each face was different

from another. Astragals, however, were less dangerous than dice, especially since the stakes were lower, such as nuts usually played for by children.
Dice, generally made from bones, were incised with progressive numbers from 1 to 6. To avoid manipulation dice were shaken in a semi-conical jugglers box (*fritillus*) and then thrown. Naturally, the winner obtained the highest points, or was he who bet on odd or even numbers coming out (*par et impar*). Other popular dice games required the use of a type of chess board (*tabula lusoria*) over which one moved a pawn (*latrunculi, calculi*) according to the number thrown on the dice.
A series of entertaining frescoes testifies to the fact that some of these inns in Pompeii were, in reality, proper gambling dens; such as the fresco painted in building VI, 10, 1 in Via di Mercurio, which shows a lively game conducted between sausages, onions and other foodstuffs suspended from beams, or that from the *caupona* VI, 14, 36, now in the National Museum of Naples. The *caupona* depicts a sequence of four scenes representing a contest between two players, made more explicit by inscriptions, which, as in cartoons, contain phrases and invective uttered by the two players. The contestants dispute the outcome, until the innkeeper intervenes by throwing them out, inviting them to quarrel outside his establishment.
In many taverns there were also prostitutes, or servants who on occasions performed this role. It was frequently heard that the owner of tavern was a pimp (*lenone*), and jurists considered taverns as "dishonest" places on a par with brothels (*Digesto*, IV, 8, 21,11).

Brothels

The number of 'houses of pleasure' in Pompeii is rather uncertain. This uncertainty is based essentially on the

fact that not all the brothels are typologically recognisable and their identification has been based, especially in the past, on elements not altogether probative, such as images and obscene graffiti. This criterion has brought to light thirty-four brothels, a disproportionate number with respect to the size of the city and the number of inhabitants. Re-evaluating this number it is possible to identify three types of brothel: that which originates solely for this purpose and is therefore built with rooms and beds in stonework such as brothel VII, 12, 18; that which has bedrooms built on the first floor of a house or tavern; and that consisting of a single room with a bed in stonework (*cella meretricia*). Although these establishments are not generally found along the main roads of the city but rather in secondary streets, their location is nevertheless conditioned by the presence of other famous public buildings. For example, in Pompeii it is possible to find particular concentrations of brothels in the vicinity of the thermal baths, such as the Forum Baths and especially near the Stabian Baths, where brothel VII,

12, 18, is a few metres from the secondary entrance.

Female prostitution

For the Romans prostitutes performed a fundamental function in defence of moral order, allowing men their freedom and guaranteeing the honesty of 'honest' women. It is no coincidence that the twin founders of Rome, Romulus and Remus, abandoned in the waters of the River Tiber because they were born out of an illegitimate union, were saved by a wolf, and *lupa* is one of the names given to prostitutes (as is the name *scortum*, which indicates prostitutes of the lowest level, who followed armies in search of clients).

Prostitution was therefore not considered a crime and prostitutes could conduct their profession freely and autonomously, selling themselves in the streets and at the crossroads called *trivia* (hence the word trivial), or as an employee of a *lenone*, in the taverns and brothels.

Prostitutes were immediately recognisable by their scanty clothing, exaggerated make-up and brightly tinted hair, preferably red or blonde.

This small erotic painting decorates the exterior of a room in the brothel of Pompeii

By means of Pompeian graffiti prostitutes speak for themselves: they express appreciation of their clients and advertise their services indicating their specialities and fees. The latter range from a minimum of two assi (the equivalent of a jug of wine) up to sixteen assi. Usually prostitutes' clients belonged to a socially modest class as the rich were able to conduct sexual relationships freely with their male and female slaves.

Prostitutes participated in the religious life of the city: the calendar provided for a holiday on the 23 April in their honour and on the 25 of the same month for their male counterparts.

Male prostitution

Roman sexual ethics did not condemn sexual intercourse between two men in itself. What was disapproved of was the fact that a man could adopt a sexually passive role. In fact, virility, in Rome, was identified with the adoption of a sexually active role, it did not matter whether with women or with men. Whoever subjected another man to sex was therefore judged as behaving normally. Males subjected by their own sex, however, were considered *mollis* (effeminate) and as such became objects of censure and heavy irony. Consequently, if a Roman male wished to have a 'virile' relationship with another man, he could chose from among his slaves or the many prostitutes who worked in the brothels, who like the women, served a male clientele. Accounts from Pompeii, however, indicate that this was not always the case. A certain Maretimus, for example, advertised his services thus: "*Maretimus cunnu liget a(ssibus) IIII. Virgins ammittit*" (Marettimus licks arses for four assi. Virgins accepted) CIL IV, 8940. This graffito, like others, does not make Pompeii a 'red-light' city: the presence of female and male prostitutes and brothels was characteristic of all Roman and Romanised cities. The legend of Pompeii as the 'city of love' (as it was once defined) must therefore be strongly refuted.

The monuments

1. The Temple of Venus
2. The Temple of Apollo
3. The Forum
4. The Basilica
5. The building of Eumachia
6. The Temple of Vespasian
7. The Macellum

8. The Forum Granary and the Weighing Table
9. The Forum Baths
10. The House of the Faun
11. The House of the Vettii
12. The Bakery
13. The Brothel
14. The Triangular Forum

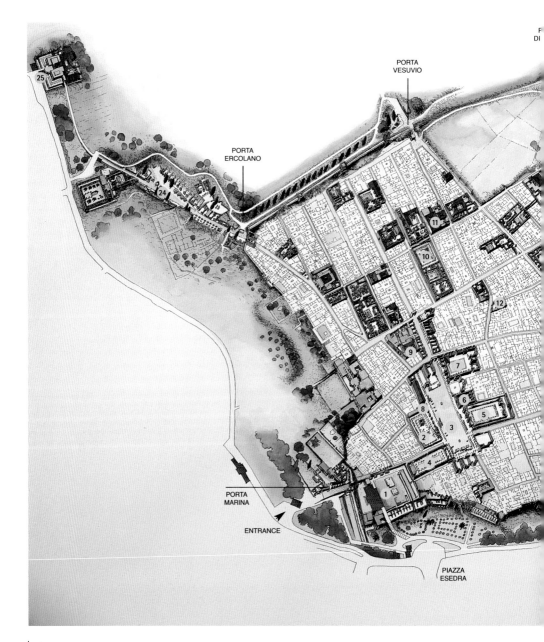

15	The Large Theatre	22	The Amphitheatre
16	The Odeion	23	The Large Palaestra
17	The Temple of Isis	24	The Necropolis of Porta Ercolano
18	The Stabian Baths	25	The Villa of the Mysteries
19	The Fullery of Stephanus		
20	The Thermopolium of L. Vetutius Placidus		
21	The House of Octavius Quartio		

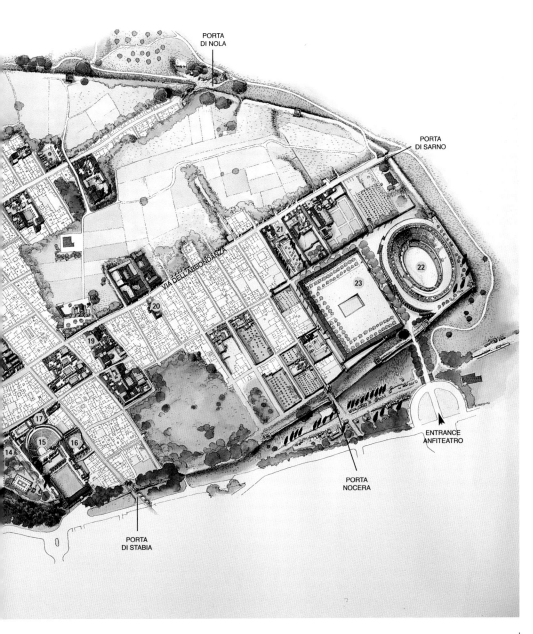

1. The Temple of Venus

With the founding of the *Colonia Cornelia Veneria Pompeianorum* on the part of Sulla in the year 80 BC, the goddess Venus became the patroness of Pompeii. Despite the importance of her cult, the temple dedicated to her worship is among the less well-known of the monuments in Pompeii. The lack of studies and information about the temple is due to the state of extreme ruin in which the building was found at the time of its excavation (1900), which is not dissimilar to that which we can still see today. Various hypotheses have been formulated regarding the reasons for such a state: some scholars maintain that the temple was undergoing demolition at the time of the eruption in 79, whilst others believe that it was still under construction. However, one of the reasons for its ruinous state was also the plunder that took place in the years immediately following 79, probably by the Pompeians who, having escaped the eruption, returned to their city to recover precious material such as the marble, which was abundant in the temple. Very little of the original building from the Sullan age remains. The arrangement of the site on a terrace and the construction of the temple on a podium, surrounded by a colonnade and probably enclosed by a wall are dated to this period. In a second phase, the sanctuary was completely renovated in the style of the splendid, marble temples of Rome that took place in the late Augustan period, before the Julio-Claudian age. The temple and adjoining site were enlarged and the marble decoration renovated.

A portico with a double row of marble columns on its eastern and western sides and a single row on its southern side surrounded the temple, with six columns at the front and three on the longest sides. (It is probable that all the colonnades consisted of two tiers). The columns, the Corinthian capitals, the denticulate cornices and the foundations that can be seen scattered throughout the site of the temple all date to this period. Badly damaged by the earthquake of 62, the sanctuary was undergoing restoration at the time of the final catastrophe.

Ivory statuette of Aphrodite, from Pompeii. National Archaeological Museum, Naples

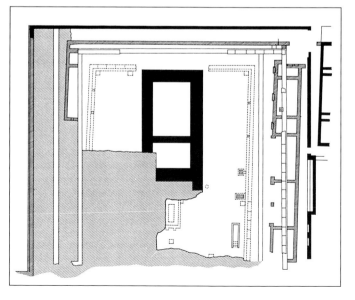

2. The Temple of Apollo

A series of essays regarding the excavations undertaken in the sacred site have demonstrated that a sanctuary dedicated to Apollo had existed there from the 6th century BC. The current arrangement however is the fruit of remarkable modifications to the temple undergone during its long life. In the 2nd century BC the ancient sanctuary was replaced by a new building conforming to Hellenistic models. The sacred site communicated directly with the Forum via a series of nine openings. During the Augustan period a sundial set on an Ionic column was placed in front of the podium, in keeping with the radiant character of the god Apollo. At about the same time the duumvirs *M. Holconius Rufus* and *C. Egnatius Posthumus* had the wall on the western side raised, and the windows of the apartments facing this side blocked up, which had evidently caused disturbance in the sanctuary. It was probably during the age of Nero that the passageways towards the Forum were closed: the temple thus remained accessible only from its southern side. The earthquake of 62 AD caused enormous damage to the sanctuary and restorations were still in progress when the eruption of 79 halted its long history forever.

The temple rises above a podium with steps in front of it (b). The cella (d), enclosed by columns with Corinthian capitals, contained the statue of the cult and the stone *omphalos*, an attribute of the Apollo of the sanctuary of Delphi, which was considered the navel of the world.

In front of the temple is the altar (a) erected during the Republican period by decree of the decurions. Opposite the portico the statue of Apollo with that of Diana in front are preserved, both represented as archers (the originals are currently on display in the National Archaeological Museum of Naples).

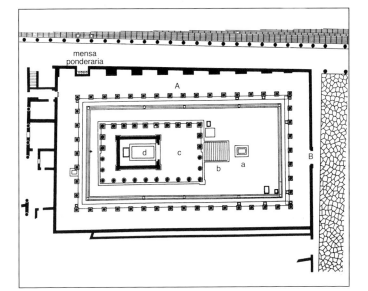

3. The Forum

The Forum square was the centre of the social, civil, commercial and religious life of the city. Situated at the crossroads of the highways leading from Naples, Nola and Stabiae it constituted a meeting and trading place from the time of its origins. During the 2nd century BC the old market place was enlarged and monumentalised; even its orientation was slightly modified. The new square, built on the Hellenistic model, featured a rectangular paved area surrounded by a portico with a double colonnade in tuff. The façade of the temple of Jupiter was centred on the longitudinal axis. Apart from the buildings of worship, the new arrangement of the square featured a series of other public buildings, the most impressive being the Basilica (monument 4). The *Macellum* (monument 7) was built in the northern sector and destined for the meat and fish markets. The eastern side had no other representative buildings; instead it was occupied by houses and taverns until the new restructuring during the Roman age. With the founding of the Roman colony, the temple of Jupiter was replaced by a temple dedicated to the Capitoline triad of deities (Jupiter, Juno and Minerva). The construction of the Building of Eumachia (monument 5), the so-called Temple of Vespasian (monument 6) and the "Sanctuary of the City Lares" date to the beginning of the Imperial age. The decision to rebuild the arcade and paving in travertine was made during the Julio-Claudian age. Not one of the numerous statues ornamenting the square, including equestrian ones, has survived: they were probably removed after the eruption of 79. Only the pedestals remain (2, 3, 4), some of which have preserved their marble coatings and dedicatory inscriptions.

The Forum, completely isolated from wheeled traffic, was closed to the north by two celebratory arches (1), which no longer bear their coatings, with statues of emperors in the niches and equestrian statues on the attic.

Three municipal buildings, whose function is still under discussion, occupied the southern side. Probably the building to the east was destined for magistrates (duumvirs), the central one for the seat of the city archives and that to the west was the aediles' hall.

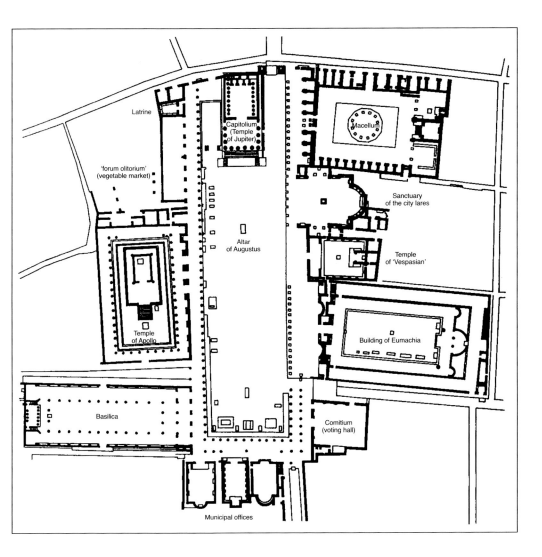

Latrine

Capitolium
(Temple
of Jupiter)

Macellum

'forum olitorium'
(vegetable market)

Sanctuary
of the city lares

Altar
of Augustus

Temple
of 'Vespasian'

Temple
of Apollo

Building of Eumachia

Basilica

Comitium
(voting hall)

Municipal offices

4. The Basilica (VIII, 1, 1-2-6)

The Basilica of Pompeii dates to the second half of the 2nd century BC and therefore constitutes the most ancient and best-preserved example of this type of building. The denomination of the word 'basilica' (from the Greek *basileios*, regal) explains the fact that such buildings had civil rather than religious functions. In fact, the Basilica was where justice was administered, trials were held and commercial transactions were completed. The layout, a rectangular area (24 x 55 metres) divided into three naves by two rows of columns, recalls the ancient Christian Basilicas. In the earliest buildings of worship, in fact, the Christians did not imitate the plan of pagan temples, which were inadequate for the religious rituals of the Christian masses, but took the plan of the Roman basilica as a model, which was more consonant with the requirements of Christian worship. The main entrance is to the east, towards the Forum, with which it communicated by means of five

doors. In line with the main entrance, on the western side is the *tribunal*, where trials were probably held. Conceived as an open gallery with two tiers of columns, Corinthian in the lower part and Ionic in the upper part, it was set on a podium about 2 metres high. The *tribunal* was completely inaccessible, since the staircases placed at either side lead to an area below the podium. It is supposed, therefore, given the vehemence of certain trials, that the central area could only be reached by means of portable wooden steps, so as to remain inaccessible and allow the trials to be conducted in peace. An alternative hypothesis is that the court may have occupied the side rooms while the central gallery acted as a sacellum and held the cult statue. There has been a long debate as to whether the building was open or covered. Nowadays the prevailing hypothesis is that the Basilica had a central roof and received light laterally through the gallery of the second tier of columns.

5. The Building of Eumachia

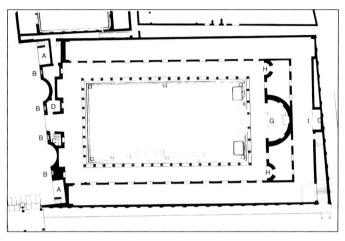

This impressive building commissioned by the rich widow Eumachia, priestess of Venus, is dedicated to the celebration of the Julio-Claudian dynasty. Two inscriptions bear witness to Eumachia's dedication; one monumental inscription placed on the architrave of the portico, the other near the side entrance on Via dell'Abbondanza, which state: "Eumachia, daughter of Lucius, public priestess, built the hall (*chalcidicum*), the covered gallery (*cryptam*) and the portico (*porticum*) in her name and that of her son M. Numistrius Fronto at her own expense: she herself dedicated it to Concordia and to Pietas Augusta." Uncertainties as to the use of this building have not yet been resolved. It may have had different uses, among which was that of a wool market. The exterior façade is animated by semicircular exedrae and by two rectangular recesses (a) accessible by staircase, where auctions were believed to be held. There are four small niches to the side of the exedrae (b): those on the left contained the statue of Romulus and Aeneas, those on the right possibly those of Caesar and Augustus.

A splendid marble frieze with twirls of acanthus, birds and insects frames the entrance door. The frieze – very probably located elsewhere originally – recalls the bas-reliefs of Ara Pacis in Rome, and has thus been attributed to Roman workmanship. Beyond the door, there are two small rooms (c and d): that on the left was used as a guardroom, that on the right contained a large terracotta pitcher designed to hold urine with which the fullers (*fullones*) bleached and worked the wool. The interior of the building was made up of a three-winged portico, with the end wing containing a large niche holding the statue of Concordia Augusta (g), probably depicted with the features of the Empress Livia. On either side there are two smaller niches (h) that probably contained the statues of Tiberius and Drusus, the sons of Livia. Small gardens were laid out in the remaining spaces behind the central niche. The walls to the east and west of the portico were furnished with small windows to allow light into the covered gallery of which the inscription speaks. At the end of the gallery was the statue of Eumachia (i) dedicated by the *fullones* to their patroness.

6. The Temple of Vespasian

The temple traditionally called of Vespasian, probably already erected in the Augustan period and therefore well before the reign of Vespasian, is a small sacred area with a tetrastyle temple on a high podium reached by two lateral staircases. The internal courtyard (F) has walls spanned by shallow niches surmounted by alternately crescent-shaped or triangular tympanums. In the centre of the courtyard is the sacrificial altar of white marble decorated on its four sides. The main side, that facing the entrance, represents the sacrifice of a bull on an altar: to the left a priest with his head covered by his cloak is reciting libations on a tripod; while at his side two young helpers (*camilli*) bring implements for the sacrifice (a jug and a bowl). Behind them are two lictors and a flute player. To the right of the tripod the *victimarius* with a two-edged axe and his assistant are bringing in the sacrificial bull. In the background a four-columned temple is depicted, which may represent the actual aedicule of the temple of Vespasian. On the north and south sides of the altar the sacred objects used during the sacrifice are represented: on the left side is an altar-cloth (*mantile*), the augural staff (*lituus*) and the box of incense (*acerra*); while on the right is a bowl (*patera*), a ladle (*simpulum*) and a jug. Above these implements is a garland of flowers and fruit. On the rear side is a crown of oak leaves.

The sacred aedicule is situated behind the altar. At the back of the cella (H) is the pedestal of the cult statue (i); the statue itself is missing, as are all the marble decorations of the aedicule. The marble may have been removed by the same Pompeians who returned to the city to recover valuable materials after the eruption of 79.

An inscription by the priestess Mamia, who dedicated a temple to the Genius of Augustus using her own funds, has been linked to this building.

7. The Macellum (VII, 9, 7)

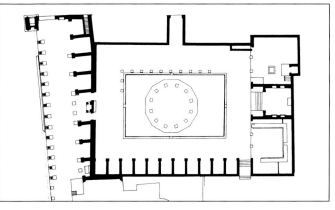

The *Macellum*, that is the market of Pompeii, rises in the north-east corner of the Forum, in order to occupy a central position in the city, but avoid disturbing the normal life of the square with the coming and going of its customers. The current building is from the Imperial age, but it replaced an earlier market, dating to the 2nd century BC. The *Macellum* consists of a huge courtyard, which was originally arcaded, with a row of shops on its southern side. There is another row of shops against the northern wall, which open however only onto the street and are not connected to the courtyard of the market.

On the side facing the entrance there are three areas that are raised with respect to the level of the market. In the centre is a small temple accessed by a ramp of five steps. Here two statues representing local dignitaries who had probably financed the construction of the building were found, while in the centre was the statue of the emperor, of which only a few fragments have been recovered. To the left is a large area containing a brick niche on a marble-covered podium, in front of which is an altar. Several different hypotheses have been advanced as to the function of this area; a sacrificial banqueting room in honour of the imperial household; a meeting room for the college of the priests of the imperial cult; and an auction room. The area to the right of this small temple was probably used for the sale of meat and fish. Fish bones and shells have been found in the sewers. Twelve tuff plinths, which served as supports, and also twelve wooden poles supporting a conical, wooden roof are in the centre of the courtyard. Below this structure (*tholos*) there was a fountain used to clean the fish. In the northern sector of the arcade a beautiful painting in the Fourth Style has been preserved. This painting has panels representing

Ulysses and Penelope, Io and Argos, and Medea who is mourning the death of her children. The side panels represent still life with birds and fish, which recall the wares sold in the market.

8. The Forum Granary and the Weighing table

The building situated in the north-western side of the Forum, almost opposite the *Macellum*, was a market for the sale of cereals and pulses. The façade has eight openings created to facilitate the coming and going of customers. At the time of the eruption of 79 it was being restored:

the portico roof and wall plastering were missing. Currently the building is being used to store archaeological findings excavated from the different areas of Pompeii. Here we can find, apart from some human plaster casts, statues, marble pieces, an olive press (*trapetum, see* the section on the *rusticae* villas) and many amphorae used to hold wine, corn, oil and *garum*.

In a recess immediately to the south of the Forum Granary is the *Mensa Ponderaria*, a marble table with nine circular cavities – from a total of twelve original ones – equivalent to different measures of capacity, utilised to inspect the fish and weigh the foodstuffs sold by the shopkeepers.

9. The Forum Baths (VII, 5, 2)

Forum Baths, tepidarium (warm room)

The Forum Baths, built at the time of the founding of the Sullan colony (80 BC), underwent several modernisations and restoration in the Julio-Claudian period. Like the Stabian Baths, the establishment was divided into two sectors, for males and females. Currently only the male sector can be visited. The entrance on Via delle Terme leads into an arcaded courtyard (A), which now houses the restaurant. One then passes into the changing room (*apodyterium*) (B), a large room with a vaulted ceiling and a mosaic floor, which has side benches in stonework for the bathers' use when changing. On the walls one can see a series of slots, evidence of the presence of wooden cupboards to hold the bathers' clothing. The *frigidarium* (C) is on the southern side, a circular area with four alcoves. The room is almost entirely occupied by a bath provided with comfortable steps for immersion in the cold water. The cornice separating the walls from

the dome is decorated with running cupids in stuccowork. From the changing room one passes into the *tepidarium* (D), where part of the rich stucco decoration of the vault completed after the earthquake of 62 AD is preserved. The room was heated by the ancient custom of braziers, still visible on the southern side. The braziers, as well as the three bronze benches at the sides, were donated by the rich Capuan industrialist *Marcus Nigidius Vaccula*; the feet of the benches and braziers are decorated with relief busts and cows' hooves alluding to his name (*vaccula* = little cow). Along the sides of the *tepidarium* are recesses flanked by telamons in stuccoed clay, which may have contained oils. Finally, one passes into the *calidarium* (E) with walls of background yellow interposed with red pillars. The vault has a wavy-patterned decoration in white stucco terminating at the impost of the vault with an open pipe to collect the water formed by the condensation of the steam: in this way the cold water did not drip back onto the bathers. The southern side has an apse containing a marble basin (*labrum*) (lb) used for rapid ablutions in cold water. On the rim of the basin there is an inscription in bronze lettering with the names of two magistrates from the Augustan age who commissioned the work. On the opposite side is the large rectangular pool for the hot bath (al), which could accommodate up to ten people. Through the gaps in the walls it is possible to see the *mammatae* tiles (tiles fitted with protuberances to distance them from the walls), and the *suspensurae* (small brick pillars) which created air ducts in the walls and flooring through which the hot stream circulated to heat the room (see the section on the thermal baths).

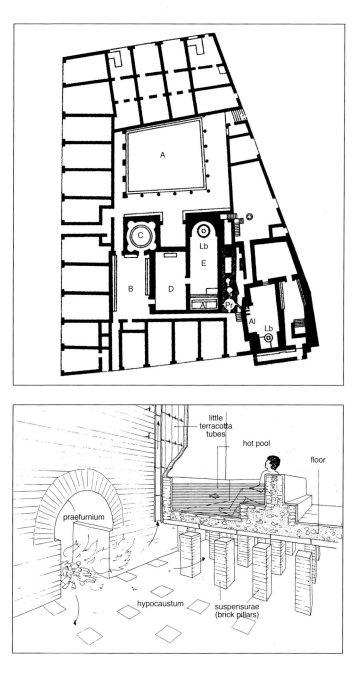

The heating system
(Adam 1989)

10. The House of the Faun (VI, 12, 2)

Cat and ducks, mosaic from the House of the Faun. National Archaeological Museum, Naples

The large Tuscan atrium with copy of statuette of Faun, original in the National Archaeological Museum, Naples

Mosaic of Alexander the Great, from the House of the Faun. National Archaeological Museum, Naples

The house, which takes its name from the statuette of the dancing faun which ornaments the impluvium (the original of which is housed in the National Archaeological Museum of Naples), was built at the beginning of the 2nd century BC on an older residence. It is considered one of the greatest examples of private residences left to us by antiquity because of its size (almost 3000 square metres) and magnificent decorations. Excavated between 1830 and 1832, very little of its original splendour has been preserved. The figured mosaics of Alexandrian inspiration have been transferred to the Archaeological Museum of Naples, while the majority of the wall decorations in the First Style have been lost. In spite of this, the importance of the house is still recognisable through its grandeur and the nobility of its architectural forms. The house has two atria, a main and a secondary one, and two peristyles. The western section is the reception area while the servants' quarters and a small private bathroom are situated in the eastern section. The bedchambers are arranged around the main atrium, at the end of which is the tablinum with a floor paved with cubes seen in perspective made of *marmo coraliticum*, a white or yellowish marble, slate and green limestone; and on either side of the atrium there are two triclinium dining rooms.

The first peristyle with an arcade of twenty-eight columns is situated behind the main atrium. At the end of the peristyle is the exedra, its mosaic threshold divided into three by the columns of the entrance and decorated with scenes of the Nile. The floor of this room was decorated with the very famous, grandiose mosaic representing the Battle of Issus between Alexander the Great and the Persian King Darius (now housed in the Archaeological Museum of Naples), and was probably created in situ with over one and a half million tesserae.

Beyond this is the second peristyle, which is much larger than the first, at the end of which are two small rooms for the gardener and two lararium recesses. A number of hypotheses regarding the identity of the owner of the house have been made, but none yet convincing. However, it is interesting to note that the Latin form of greeting 'HAVE', has been written in mosaics on the pavement in front of the entrance, which is somewhat perplexing because it dates to the period (the Sullan age) when the language spoken in Pompeii was still Oscan. This has led to the hypothesis that the owner of the house was a Roman or Latin who installed himself in Pompeii early on, and who imported a more evolved typology of housing into the Campanian city.

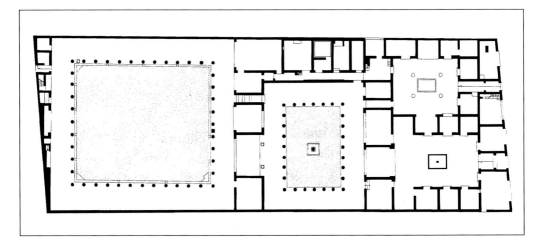

11. The House of the Vettii (VI, 15, 1)

Wine-merchant cupids, fresco in the hall

The atrium and the 'oecus' (living room) decorated in the Fourth Style

The house was excavated in 1894 and simultaneously furnished with a roof, which allowed the paintings of the Fourth Style to be preserved. The house, with a rather ancient structure, was restructured around the middle of the 1st century AD, probably on occasion of its purchase by the two wealthy Vettii brothers, who belonged to the class of freedmen. On entering, the right–hand doorjamb has a representation of Priapus with an enormous phallus laid on one pan of a pair of scales, while the counterweight pan holds a full moneybag. The function of the painting is to ward off the evil eye and to augur prosperity to the occupants of the house. In the atrium, to the right and left are two iron coffers with bronze nails and ornaments anchored to a stonework pedestal. The decoration of the atrium is particularly refined. On the skirting board one can see children making sacrifices in honour of the Penates, the gods who were traditionally worshipped in the atrium; and in the frieze above there are cupids absorbed in various games.

A number of rooms open onto the atrium. The bedchamber is decorated with representations of various types of prized edible fish and the *oecus* (living room) is decorated with mythological scenes (Cyparissus who has killed Apollo's favourite deer is on the entrance wall and the fight between Eros and Pan is on the end wall). On the northern side of the atrium are the servants' quarters with a small atrium, which has a sumptuous lararium on the left-hand wall with the *Genio* (spiritual protector) of the householder between two Lares. Inside is the kitchen with bronze pans on tripods on the cooking range where they were found in situ. Opposite the kitchen is a small, decorated room of uncertain use. In the residential sector of the house, the peristyle, which encloses an elegant garden, has been given special development and recomposed according to its original arrangement. The garden is richly adorned with marble and bronze statues (some of which are copies) and pools for water displays. The reception rooms open onto the peristyle: the triclinium is decorated with false architectural perspectives, small pictures of naval battles and mythological scenes

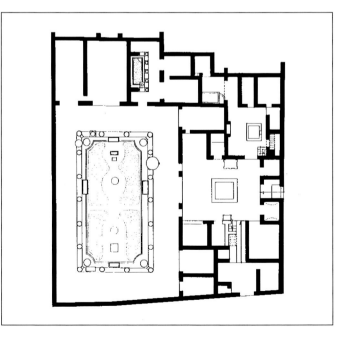

(Daedalus and Pasiphae to the left, Ixion tied to the wheel on the end wall, and Dionysus and Ariadne to the right); the *oecus* with the famous frieze of cupids and *psychai* (little images of souls) engaged in various trades (flower and perfume vendors, goldsmiths, laundry workers and vine harvesters) and sporting activities (chariot racing with antelopes); and the *oecus* with decorations on a yellow background, perspective partitions and mythological scenes (baby Hercules strangling the snakes on the left, Pentheus being killed by the Bacchantes on the end wall and the punishment of Dirce to the right).

12. The Bakery
VII, 2, 22

During the 2nd century BC the home baking of bread was replaced almost completely by industrial production. Thus, numerous bakeries (*pistrina*) opened in Pompeii, as in other Roman cities (see the section on commerce), such as this one probably run by a freedman *N. Popidius Priscus*. This establishment, in contrast to others in the city, did not have a baker's shop, and the wholesale distribution of bread was entrusted to a group of itinerant peddlers.

Along the right-hand walls three table supports in stonework remain, probably used to rest the round loaves on. In the centre of the bakery, which is paved with slabs of lavic stone, are four mills arranged in a row and two smaller ones a short distance away. The mills made from a dark grey, lavic stone are porous and very resistant. They consist of a fixed, conical-shaped, lower part (*meta*) and a mobile upper part of two cone shapes, with a hollow cylinder on the inside (*catillus*). In the narrow part of the *catillus* a bar was inserted and occasionally pushed by manpower, but more frequently by animals, thereby creating the rotary motion. In this way the grain which was poured into the upper cavity of the *catillus* was ground in the lower half, where it came out as flour to be collected on the circular base below, which was protected by thin plates of lead or wood. On the left is the oven with a conical hood, its opening surrounded by lavic stone to resist knocks from the baker's shovel, and which was closed by an iron door. On the floor to the right of the oven one can see the remains of a water container, used either to sprinkle the half-cooked loaves of bread to obtain a shiny crust, or to cool the oven shovel.

13. The Brothel
(VII, 12, 18-20)

The brothel, run perhaps, in the last years of the life of the city, by two partners *Africanus* and *Victor*, has three entrances. The first two (nos. 18-19 of Via del Lupanare) are on the ground floor and lead into an area consisting of a corridor with five rooms opening onto it. Each of the rooms has a bed with a stonework shelf, on which the mattress was laid. At the end of the corridor is a small latrine screened by a low wall. There are erotic frescoes at the entrance of each room, which explicitly illustrate different sexual positions (*figurae Veneris*). To the right of the main entrance is a representation of Priapus with two phalli. About one hundred and twenty graffiti by prostitutes and clients have been found inside the rooms. At the end of each room, screened by a low wall, is a small latrine.

The entrance at number 20, with its own door and bell, leads into another five rooms situated on the upper floor. These rooms are more spacious than those on the floor below and enjoyed greater privacy.

14. The Triangular Forum and the Doric Temple (VIII, 7, 30)

A wide space, which took on a triangular shape to adapt itself to the lava crest on which it rises, has been the site of an ancient Doric Temple since the 4th century BC. During the second half of the 2nd century BC the area was improved by the addition of arcades and inserted into the new urban scheme applied to the theatres.

Access to the Forum was through a monumental entrance hall preceded by a gateway with Ionic columns. The space is limited on the inside by a Doric colonnade. Along the eastern side, the arcade communicates with a small gymnasium and another two passageways lead to the semi-circular exterior of the Large Theatre. The temple, which rises at the end of the area, was probably dedicated to Hercules and Minerva. The temple is in a state of almost total ruin, for the most part due to previous alterations, but in part also to the archaeological excavations. Only the foundations and a series of architectonic terracotta of archaic and Samnitic

age survive, which were found amongst the samples of the excavation.

15. The Large Theatre

Despite extensive restorations undertaken during the Augustan age, the theatre of Pompeii, built in the 2nd century BC, preserves its essentially Greek appearance.
As in all Greek theatres, it was erected by resting part of the steps (*cavea*) against the slope of the hill. The horseshoe shaped *cavea* is divided into three zones horizontally called *ima, media* and *summa cavea*, and they in turn are sub-divided radially into five wedges (*kerkides*). The *ima cavea*, nearest to the stage and with larger seats, was reserved for the authorities; the *media cavea* was probably destined for eminent dignitaries of the city and representatives of the artisan guilds. Other members of the public were distributed between the *media* and *summa cavea*. It appears that women occupied the highest part of the theatre. Public access was by two passageways, which were covered during the

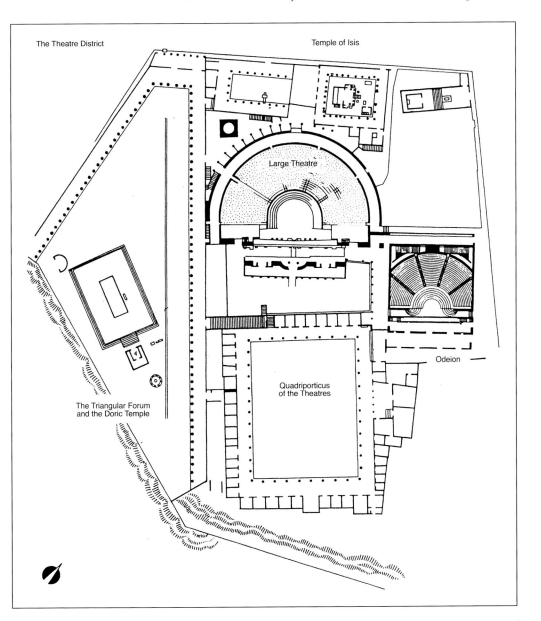

The Theatre District

Temple of Isis

Large Theatre

Odeion

The Triangular Forum
and the Doric Temple

Quadriporticus
of the Theatres

Augustan age, called *parodoi*, and situated at the extremities of the hemisphere. The front of the stage (*proskenion*) rests directly on the walls of the *parodoi*. Here it is still possible to see the encasing of the wooden beams where the curtain lodged, which was not let down from above, as in modern theatres, but was lifted from below.

The stage, the backdrop to the performances, was equipped with a central apse and two rectangular recesses on either side and was originally ornamented by columns and marble statues. There is a large area behind the stage, connected to it by three doors, which was probably used as the actors' changing room. Following the restorations in the Augustan age undertaken by the architect *Marcus Artorius Primus*, the capacity of the theatre was increased to hold up to five thousand spectators. Behind the theatre is a large quadrangular area with arcades, which functioned as a *foyer*, where spectators could stroll during the long intervals of the performances.

16. The Odeion (The Small Theatre)

Next to the theatre is the *Odeion*, a covered building with a smaller structure to reduce the dispersion of sound, which was used for musical performances, recitations, mime and probably recitals of poetry and literature as well. The Odeion could hold about one thousand five hundred spectators. It was built during the first half of the 1st century BC at the instigation of two magistrates, followers of Sulla.

The *Odeion* is subdivided into an *ima* and *media cavea* but has no *summa*. The last row of the *ima cavea* is closed by a balustrade terminating in winged, leonine paws. The walls surrounding the *cavea* are decorated at their ends with telamons in tuff. The steps are shaped to ensure greater comfort for the spectators: the front part, somewhat raised, acted as a seat, while the rear part was used both as a passageway and as a footrest for the row of spectators behind. The orchestra was not horseshoe

shaped, as in the Large Theatre, but semi-circular. The back walls of the stage and the floor of the orchestra were covered in marble during the Augustan age, the work commissioned by the duumvir *M. Oculatius Verus*, as shown by the inscription in bronze characters in the flooring. The building has not undergone major alterations and preserves, more than the Large Theatre nearby, the stamp of the late-Hellenistic architectural tradition.

17. The Temple of Isis

The sanctuary was brought to light between the years 1764 and 1766, and stripped of the statues and the extraordinary paintings that decorated it, according to the system adopted during the Bourbon period. The paintings and treasures are exhibited in a room that was recently set up at the National Museum of Naples. An inscription placed above the entrance doorway (this is a copy, the original being housed in the Museum of Naples) provides valuable information regarding the history of the Temple. The inscription makes reference to the goddess worshipped, Isis, to the fact that the complex was reconstructed *ex novo* after the earthquake in 62, and to the name of its munificent constructor, *N. Popidius Celsinus*, a child of only six years old. His father, the freedman *N. Popidius Ampliatus*, unable to become a decurion himself due to his previous condition of slavery, believed that this act of munificence would launch his son on a political career. All the elements in tuff date to the original temple erected at the end of the 2nd century BC, while the remaining elements belong to the aforementioned post-seismic reconstruction. The temple, in the centre of a courtyard with colonnades, is constructed with lateritious bricks on a high podium, with four frontal columns and two lateral ones. In the cella is a high pedestal for a statue, of which only a few fragments have been found. Behind, on the external wall, a small recess was hollowed out flanked by two ears made of stucco, indicating the willingness of the goddess to listen to the prayers of her followers. Two other recesses are next to the cella and probably contained the statues of Harpocrates and Anubis, the god with the head of a jackal. Apart from the temple, there are other buildings of worship in the courtyard in honour of the Egyptian goddess. In the south-eastern corner is the *purgatorium*, used as its name suggests, for purification ceremonies, which took place using water from the Nile, which was preserved in a large urn. Behind the temple is a huge area, the *ecclesiastèrion*, reserved for meetings of the initiates to the mysteries of Isis and probably for sacred performances as well. The area was decorated with large paintings depicting ritual landscapes and myths, which are now housed in the National Museum of Naples.

18. The Stabian Baths (VII, 1, 8)

Stucco decoration of the ceiling, detail

Room with under-floor heating

Frigidarium, round bathing room with cold pool

This is the oldest thermal complex of Pompeii. The original nucleus dates back to the 4th century and consists of a series of rooms with pools for individual baths, of which some have survived in the north-western area of the complex. Subsequently the building underwent remarkable changes. During the 2nd century BC the complex was transformed into a public bath and divided into male and female sections. Subsequent additions and restorations were made during the early years of the colony (80-70 BC). Damaged by the earthquake of 62, the building had only been partially restored at the time of the eruption in 79.

The main entrance (a), on Via dell'Abbondanza, leads into a huge enclosure dominated by the palaestra of trapezoidal shape (b), bounded on three sides by an arcade. To the west of the palaestra, on the side without an arcade, is the cold pool built around the middle of the 1st century BC. On either side of the room containing the pool are two areas (c) containing fountains, which were probably used by clients for a preliminary wash before immersion in the pool. To the south is another room that was probably used as a changing room. The external walls of these rooms are richly decorated in stucco dating to the last years of the life of the city. They represent perspective architecture in which various characters have been inserted (Jupiter with a sceptre and an eagle, a satyr offering a drunk Hercules a drink, and wrestlers cleaning themselves with strigils).

The thermal bathing rooms are on the eastern side. Only the male section can be visited. One enters a vestibule with a barrel-vaulted ceiling decorated with polychrome stucco. On the left is a circular room probably transformed in the Augustan period into a *frigidarium* (e), and almost completely occupied by the cold pool. From the vestibule one passes into the *apodyterium* (f), furnished with benches in stonework along the walls for waiting and to facilitate changing, and with stonework recesses to leave clothing. The vault and lunette of this room are richly decorated with polychrome stucco. On the left is the entrance to the *tepidarium* (g) (closed to the public) and from here access to the *calidarium* with a washbasin for ablutions on the recessed side and a pool for the hot bath on the opposite side (h).

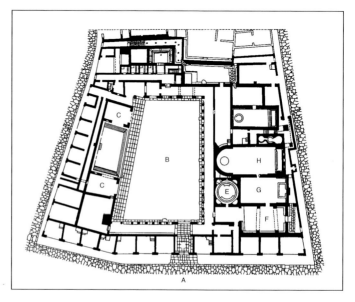

19. The Fullery of Stephanus (I, 6,7)

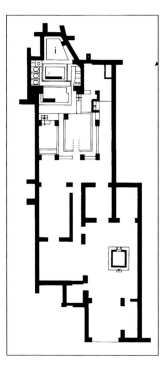

Excavated in 1911, this fullery is the best of the four large *fullonicae* preserved out of a total of eighteen identified in Pompeii. *Fullonicae* performed more functions than normal laundries; both the removal of fat from the cloth before it was sold and the washing and the removal of stains from dirty clothes took place here. A well-cleaned, white toga conferred a sign of distinction that the Romans held dear. The *fullonica* of *Stefanus*, named after an electoral manifesto found on the façade bearing this name, was created by transforming an ancient house with an atrium. The impluvium was utilised for the construction of a tank with parapets, probably used to wash the most delicate cloth. A skylight replaced the compluvium. The roof is the only example of a flat roof in a house with an atrium in Pompeii. It may have been built this way to exploit the large terrace to hang out the washing. Behind the peristyle three tanks were built, set at different levels and interconnected by holes in the walls. The tanks have no drainage outlets, so we assume that they were emptied by buckets or siphons. The tanks had built-in steps allowing the *fullones* (fullers) to step down inside to rinse the cloth. On the left there are three oval basins and on the right two other basins and another similar receptacle. The cloth was trampled in these containers in water and soda or other alkaline substances such as human or animal urine, which were kept in amphorae without necks and left intentionally in the aisles or entrance of the fullery (see the chapter on the economy). The Emperor Vespasian levied a tax on the collection of urine for industrial purposes (Svetonius, *Vitae Caesarum, Vespasian*, 23).

Hardened by this liquid, the cloth was subsequently treated with fullers' clay, after which it was beaten and rinsed in the three large tanks. In the space marked (i) there is a kitchen, where meals were prepared for the workers of the *fullonica*. An entire battery of saucepans was found here on the stove and hanging on the walls. On the left there is a latrine.

20. The Thermopolium of L. Vetutius Placidus (I, 8, 8)

This building is one of many commercial establishments situated on Via dell'Abbondanza, destined for the sale of food and hot drinks. On the basis of inscriptions painted on the façade of the building and those found on three amphorae discovered in the garden, the owner of the house and manager of the thermopolium has been identified as *Lucius Vetutius* (or *Betutius) Placidus.*

The thermopolium is characterised by a three-sided counter covered in polychrome marble in which the *dolia* (big terracotta vases), containing food or hot drinks, were encased. In one of these *dolia* a large sum of money was found, all in small change: 374 assi and 1,237 quadrants, to a total value of 683 sestertii. The sum appears to be too high to represent the takings of a single day, so it may have been from sales in the final days preceding the eruption. In the centre of the eastern side there are traces of a small oven used to heat or prepare the food and hot drinks. On the wall at the back there is a beautiful, painted lararium, with the *Genius* in the act of making a sacrifice on a tripod, flanked by the Lares. At the two ends are Mercury, the god of commerce and protector of thieves, with a caduceus and a bag of money in his left hand; and on the extreme right Dionysus, the god of wine, with a panther by his side. From the thermopolium one passes into a room, which may have been a triclinium, probably destined for clients who did not wish to eat their meals standing. Behind the thermopolium was the owner's home with paintings in the Third Style.

21. The House of Octavius Quartio (also called of Loreius Tiburtinus) (II, 2, 2)

Originally the house was much larger (2770 square metres), including the adjacent residence (II, 2, 4). After the year 62 the two nuclei were separated. On entering it is interesting to note the tracing of the two-panelled door rotating on hinges set in the threshold, complete with bronze and iron knockers which decorated the exterior side. In the atrium, in place of the impluvium, which was progressively losing its importance, was a fountain ornamented with flowers and plants. In the interior of the house is the richly painted *oecus*: the skirting board is in imitation marble, followed by a low frieze depicting the deeds of Achilles and a second frieze higher up representing the expedition of Hercules against Laomedon, King of Troy. However, the most characteristic element of the house is the area destined as the garden, which is highly innovative in its design of watercourses. There are two channels arranged as a T: the first, parallel to the area of the house, is connected at one end to the biclinium for open-air meals, and to a nymphaeum with a pumice-lined recess, from which the water spouted. Around the aedicule are representations of myths connected with water (Narcissus gazing at his reflection and Pyramus' suicide near a spring), painted by the artist *Lucius*, who left the only artist's signature found in Pompeii. At the time of the excavations the water channel was found surrounded by marble statues representing various Egyptian themes (animals, divinities, sphinxes and Muses). The second channel begins on a lower level, from a nymphaeum under the small temple of four columns, which, articulated in several pools with water jets, crosses the entire garden and orchard and permits irrigation. In the '30s the careful work of excavation allowed the reconstruction of the scenographic garden, thanks also to plaster casts of the trees. Recently trees and vines have been replanted and the long wooden pergolas have been reconstructed.

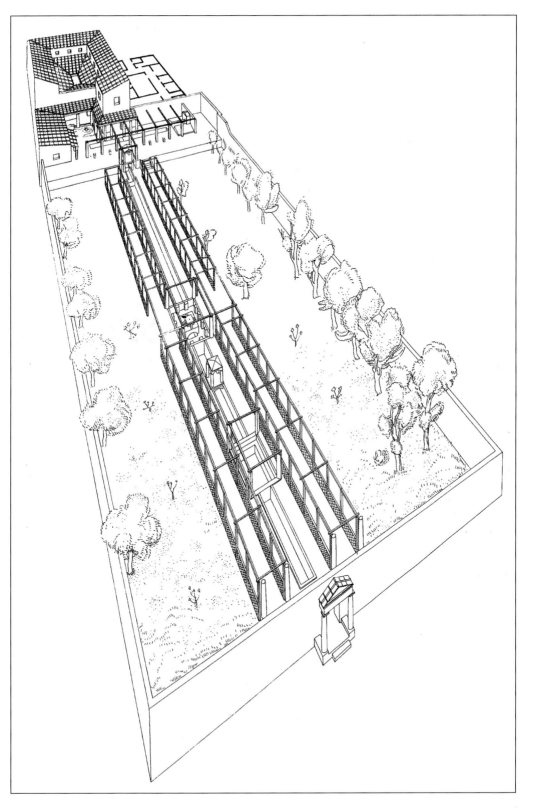

22. The Amphitheatre

The amphitheatre of Pompeii, constructed shortly after '80 BC, is amongst the oldest buildings used for gladiatorial contests that has come down to us. It was built in an area of the city that was relatively free of buildings, and decentralised so that the crowds of people – coming in from neighbouring cities as well – would not create traffic congestion. The building was partly constructed against the fortifying ring of the city walls. An artificial embankment was also created by a buttressed wall with a façade of blind arches. That which differentiates this building from the most common type of amphitheatre, is the lack of subterranean areas under the floor of the arena. Other unusual elements are the access points to the *summa cavea*, which was reached by steps that were leant against the exterior of the building. The upper gallery appears to have been reserved for women, according to an Augustan ordinance. The most privileged seats reserved for magistrates on the lower steps and the *media cavea* were reached by means of a covered gallery accessible from two passageways located on the western side. Another two passageways located respectively to the south and north of the gallery lead directly into the arena. Large stone rings were found along the upper parapet of the gallery, in which wooden beams were fitted, maintaining on sliding ropes the large, linen curtain (*velarium*) used to protect the spectators from the sun. This is confirmed not only by certain public notices advertising the games, but also by the famous fresco reproducing the amphitheatre during the riot between the Pompeians and Nocerines in 59 AD (now in the Naples Archaeological Museum). Following this episode the arena was 'disqualified' for ten years, but after the earthquake of 62, the Emperor Nero revoked the ban. The amphitheatre could hold about 20,000 spectators.

Gladiator helmet from Pompeii. National Archaeological Museum, Naples

23. The Large Palaestra

The Large Palaestra, situated opposite the Amphitheatre, was built during the Augustan age under the impetus of imperial politics, and designed to promote physical exercise together with *virtus* among the youth of the upper classes. The Palaestra is a huge rectangular area (107 x 141 metres) surrounded by a three-winged portico and enclosed by high walls, which were originally battlements. The main façade opens with three entrances on the side of the Amphitheatre, other entrances are found on the northern, eastern and western sides.

In the centre there is a large pool (34.55 x 22.25 metres) constructed on an incline with a depth varying from 1 to 2.60 metres. There were plane trees of over a hundred years old growing at the sides of the Palaestra at the time of the eruption, which can be seen by their plaster casts.

A large number of graffiti have been found along the walls of the portico and on the columns, many of which refer to the amphitheatre games, and there is no lack of obscene comments or even personal feelings which paint a vivid picture of the life that took place there.

Victory, bronze statuette from Pompeii. National Archaeological Museum, Naples. Probably the statuette held a crown in the right hand. The crown was a symbol of victory in the athletic games

The Large Palaestra in a 19th century etching

24. The Necropolis of Porta Ercolano (Via dei Sepolcri)

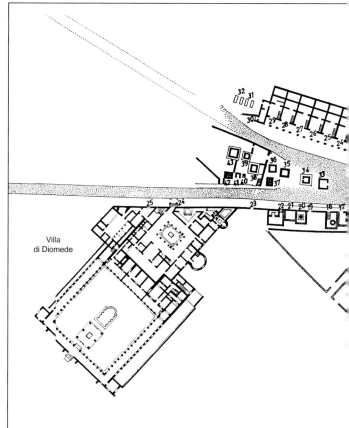

Tomb of the priestess Mamia, with a semicircular base ('schola'). The tomb behind it belonged to the Istacidii, one of the most important Pompeian families, owners of the Villa of the Mysteries

The necropolis, excavated between the years 1763 and 1838, is situated immediately outside Porta Ercolano (the Herculaneum Gate), along the road from Naples. The tombs, which are laid out on both sides of the road, alternate with aristocratic villas and *tabernae* (shops). There are various types of tombs represented in the necropolis, demonstrating a wide typology of funerary architecture of the Roman period. The tombs rarely belong to an individual: in the majority of cases they held several members of the same family, their servants and freedmen. Cremation was the most widespread funeral rite, the ashes being preserved in urns of terracotta, glass or marble and deposited in special loculi arranged along the walls of the vault of the tomb.

The western side (on the left leaving Porta Ercolano)

Tomb 1:
Recessed tomb of the Augustale *M. Cerrinus Restitutus*, of the Flavian period.
Tomb 2:
Tomb with semi-circular exedra (*schola*) belonging to *Aulo Veio*.
Tomb 3:
Sepulchre of *M. Porcio*, probably the same person who had the Odeion and Amphitheatre of Pompeii built.
Tomb 4:
Schola tomb dedicated to Mamia, priestess of Venus, as written on the inscription on the backrest.
Tomb 4b:
Mausoleum of the *Istacidi* family built on a high podium containing the sepulchral chamber, crowned on the

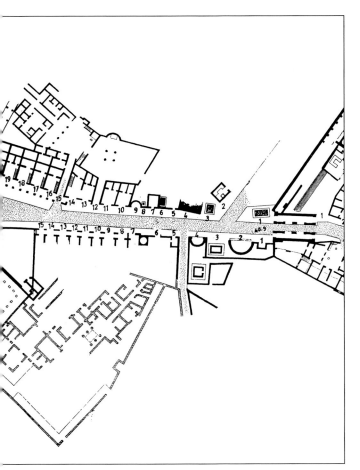

continues towards the Villa of the Mysteries. Returning, on the other side of the road, there is another series of tombs after a colonnaded building with a series of *tabernae* at the front.

The eastern side

Tomb 9:
Sepulchre of semicircular recesses with a seat inside for wayfarers to rest, painted and decorated in stucco.
Tomb 8:
Inside the small sepulchral chamber there were three cremation urns, one of terracotta and two of glass, one of which was the very famous Blue Vase, the urn with cupids harvesting grapes, now housed in the National Museum of Naples.
Tomb 6:
Tomb with a high quadrangular podium elegantly decorated with garlands.
Tomb 2:
Tomb with a funerary enclosure belonging to the aedile *Titus Terentius Felix.*
Tomb 1:
Tomb in the form of a large altar.

upper part by a small, circular temple that held the statues of the most important members of the family. Following this tomb is the façade of the so-called Villa of Cicero with a portico and *tabernae.*
Tomb 16:
Unfinished tomb at the time of the eruption of 79.
Tomb 17:
Tomb with a high stucco enclosure with representations of gladiatorial contests, probably belonging to *Umbricius Scaurus*, a well-known producer of *garum*, the famous fish sauce.
Tomb 18:
Circular mausoleum on a quadrangular podium surrounded by an enclosure.
Tomb 20:
Tomb with an altar resting on a stepped pyramid, surrounded

by an enclosure, belonging to the Augustale *Caio Calventio Quieto*.
Tomb 22:
Cenotaph erected by *Naevoleia Tyche*, whose portrait is above the inscription, for herself, her husband *C. Munatius Fausto*, and for their freedmen. On the side panels of the altar are representations of the *bisellium* (the chair of honour) and a ship entering a port, symbolising the journey of the soul.
Tomb 23:
Tomb in the form of a funerary triclinium, dedicated to *Cnaeus Vibius Saturninus.*
Other funerary monuments are in the centre of the area, in the space between the bifurcation of the two roads, among which is the sepulchre of the *gens Arria*, decorated with fascia in bas-relief. The road

25. The Villa of the Mysteries

Built in the 2nd century BC as a luxury villa on the outskirts of the city, it underwent a transformation around 60 BC and finally had a rustic quarter added to it in the 1st century BC.
The villa probably belonged to the influential *Istacidii* family, as testified by the discovery there of a ring with a seal. The present entrance is on the opposite side of the original one (a). In line with the entrance is the peristyle (b) used to connect the residential and servants' quarters. Continuing to the left one reaches the kitchen and on the right there is an area where two wine presses are preserved (see the section on the *villae rusticae*).
The residential section faced the sea. The rooms are arranged around the atrium and are mainly decorated with

frescoes in the Second Style, dating back to the restructuring which took place around 60 BC.

The villa is called the "Villa of the Mysteries" after the famous series of paintings, deriving from Hellenistic models, which decorate salon (c), which are believed to represent an initiation rite to the Dionysian mysteries. The rite was a mystery revealed only to members of the sect, and it was this secrecy that aroused the suspicions of the Roman state authorities, to the point of issuing a *senatus consultum* (a senatorial decree) with which they banned the Bacchanalian revels (186 BC).

The significance of the fresco in the triclinium still remains in reality a 'mystery'. From the time of its discovery, at the beginning of the 20th century, numerous hypotheses have been made regarding the significance of the images represented there, and the debate continues.

The *megalographia* (big panting) – the name given by Vitruvius to compositions of this genre – is composed of almost life-sized figures, represented on a high podium, as if they were theatrical figures.

The interpretation seems to proceed from left to right. The first group consists of two women and a child who is reading, believed by many scholars to represent a young Dionysus. This is followed by another female figure carrying a bowl of fruit or cooked food. The subsequent group consists of three women around a table, interpreted at times as the personification of three Seasons, at others as a priestess (the central figure with her back turned) and her attendants. The next group consists of an elderly Silenus, crowned with bay leaves and with a lyre, and of two shepherds with two goats. There follows a majestic female figure holding the hem of her cloak billowing with air, identified by some as Aura, personification of the wind, and unwilling mother to Dionysus. In the next group the old Silenus reappears,

crowned with ivy, with a small satyr or small, female Pan figure, who is drinking (or looking into the bottom the cup?) and another who is raising a mask. The next scene, full of gaps, shows perhaps an inebriated Dionysus in the arms of Ariadne.

The following group shows a woman bending over in the act of unveiling a phallus, symbol of the generative force of nature, and a winged female form with a long staff, alluding perhaps to the flagellation, a common rite in the Dionysian religion.

The following scene shows a crouching woman sheltering in the arms of a lady who seems to be protecting her (perhaps from whipping by the winged figure?). On the right there is a naked female dancer with cymbals behind which is a feminine figure with a thyrsus. In the next scene a beautiful young girl is sitting combing her hair, and she is almost unanimously acknowledged as a bride separating her hair into six locks according to the hairstyle in fashion for the marriage ritual. The last figure, isolated in the corner between the two doors, is a seated woman, believed to be the representation of the *Domina*, the mistress of the house.

Bibliography

*The bibliography, without being
exhaustive, is intended to provide
only a bibliographic orientation
to the topics presented in this volume.*

Introduction to the history
and archaeology of Pompeii

AA.VV., *Volcanologie et Archéologie,
Actes des Ateliers Européens de
Ravello 1987 e 1989*, in 'PACT' 25,
1990.
C. Albore Livadie (ed.),
*Tremblements de terre, éruptions
volcaniques et vie des hommes dans la
Campanie antique*, Napoli 1986
J. Andreau, *Histoire des séismes et
histoire économique. Le tremblement
de terre de Pompei, 62, ap. J.C.*, in
'AnnEconSocCiv' 28, 1973,
pp. 369-395.
F. Bologna, *Le scoperte di Ercolano e
Pompei nella cultura europea del
XVIII secolo*, in 'La Parola del
Passato', 34, Fasc.188-189, 1979,
pp. 377- 404.
R. Cantilena, *Vizi privati e pubbliche
virtù. Il gabinetto degli oggetti
riservati del Museo di Napoli*, in
L'Amore. Dall'Olimpo all'alcova,
Milano 1992, pp. 51-60.
E. Corti, *Ercolano e Pompei*, reprint,
V ed., 1977.
E. De Carolis, *Testimonianze
archeologiche in area vesuviana
posteriori al 79 d.C.*, in 'Archeologia,
uomo, territorio' 16, Milano 1997,
pp. 17-32.
T. Fröhlich, L. Jacobelli (ed.)
*Archaologie und Seismologie. La
regione vesuviana dal 62 al 79 d.C.
Problemi archeologici e sismologici*,
München 1995.
R.A. Genovese, *Giuseppe Fiorelli e la
tutela dei beni culturali dopo l'unità
d'Italia*, Napoli 1992.

E. Guidobaldi (ed.), *I terremoti
prima del Mille in Italia e nell'area
mediterranea*, Bologna 1989.
I. Jenkins- K. Sloan, *Vases and
Volcanoes. Sir William Hamilton and
his collection*, London 1996.
A. Luisi, *L'esplosione del Vesuvio del
79 d.C.*, in M. Sordi (ed.), *Fenomeni
naturali e avvenimenti storici
nell'antichità,* Milano 1989, pp. 227-
236.
O. Onorato, *La data del terremoto di
Pompei: 5 febbraio 62 d.C.*, in
'Rend.Lincei' 8, Ser. 4, 1949,
pp. 644-661.
M. Pagano, *Testimonianze post 79
nell'area vesuviana*, in 'Rivista di
Studi Pompeiani' VII (1995-1996),
1998, pp. 35-44.
E. Renna, *Vesuvius Mons. Aspetti del
Vesuvio nel mondo antico tra filologia
archeologia vulcanologia*, Napoli,
1992.
F. Sigurdsson, S. Carey, W. Cornell,
T. Pescatore, *The Eruption of
Vesuvius in A.D. 79*, in 'Nat. Geog.
Res.', 1, 1985, 332-387.
G. Soricelli, *La regione vesuviana
dopo l'eruzione del 79 d.C.*, in
'Atheneum', LXXXV, 1, 1997,
pp. 139-154.
F. Zevi (ed.), *Pompei 79. Raccolta di
studi per il decimonono centenario
dell'eruzione vesuviana*, Napoli 1979.
F. Zevi (ed.) *Pompei*, I-II, Napoli
1991-1992.

Family life and the condition
of women

E. Cantarella, *Pompei. I volti
dell'amore*, Toledo, 1998.
M. D'Avino, *La donna a Pompei*,
Napoli, 1964.
S. Dixon, *The Roman Family*,
Baltimore-London 1992.
J.F. Gardner, *Women in Roman Law

and Society*, Bloomington-
Indianapolis, 2nd edition, 1990.
L. Peppe, *Posizione giuridica e ruolo
sociale della donna romana in età
repubblicana,* Roma 1984.
B. Rawson (ed.), *Marriage, Divorce
and Children in Ancient Rome*,
Canberra-Oxford, 1991
C. Savunen, *Women and Elections in
Pompeii*, in R. Halwey, B. Levick,
Women in Antiquity, London-New
York, 1995.
EAD., *Women in the urban texture of
Pompeii*, Helsinki 1997.
P. Virgili, *Acconciature e maquillage*,
(Vita e costumi dei Romani Antichi,
7), Roma 1989.

Politics

P. Castrén, *L'amministrazione
municipale*, in *Pompei 79*, cit., p. 45ff.
F. De Martino, *Storia della
costituzione romana,* Napoli. 1973
S.L. Dyson, *Age, Sex and Status: the
View from the Roman Rotary Club*,
in *Echos du monde classique /
Classical Views*, XXXVI, n.s.11,
1992, p. 369ff.
ID., *Community and Society in
Roman Italy*, Baltimore, 1992.
J.L. Franklin, *Pompeii: The Electoral
Programmata, Campaigns and Politics
A.D. 71-79*, Roma 1980.
ID. *Games and a Lupanar:
Prosopography of a neighborhood in
Ancient Pompeii*, in *C.J.* 81, 1986,
p. 319ff.
E. Lepore, *Orientamenti per la storia
sociale di Pompei*, in 'Pompeiana',
Napoli 1950, p. 144ff.
E. Lo Cascio, *La società pompeiana
dalla città sannitica alla colonia
romana*, in F. Zevi (ed.), *Pompei 1*,
Napoli, 1992, p. 113 ff.
E. Magaldi, *La guerra sociale: suoi
riflessi e sue consequenze a Pompei*, in

'Rivista di Studi Pompeiani' II, 1936-37, p. 43ff.
W. Moeller, *The Riot of A.D. 59 at Pompeii*, in 'Historia' 19, 1970, p. 84ff.
P. Moreau, *Sur le murs de Pompei, Choix d'Inscriptions latines*, Paris, 1993.
H. Mouritsen, *Elections, Magistrates and Municipal Elite. Studies in Pompeian Epigraphy*, Roma 1988.
O. Onorato, *Pompei municipium e colonia romana*, in 'Rend. Acc. Napoli', n.s. XXVI, 1951, p. 115ff.
R.A. Staccioli (ed.), *Manifesti elettorali nell'antica Pompei,* Milano 1992.
A. Varone, *L'amministrazione della città e la vita pubblica*, in *Pompei. Decorazioni parietali della città sepolta*, Torino-London, 1997, p. 21ff.

The Economy

M.C. Amouretti, *Le pain et l'huile dans la Grèce antique*, Paris 1986.
J. Andreau, *Remarques sur la société pompéienne*, in 'Dialoghi d'Archeologia' VII, 1973, p. 213ff.
ID., *Les affaires de Monsieur Jucundus*, Roma 1974.
ID., *Pompei: enchères, foires et marchés*, in 'Bulletin de la Societé Nationale des Antiquaires de France', 1976, p. 104ff.
R. Angelone, *L'officina coactiliaria di M. Vecilio Verecundo a Pompei*, Napoli, 1986.
B. Borecky, *La lavorazione della farina e del pane a Pompei*, in *Un contributo alla storia economica di Pompei nel I sec.d.C.*, 'UDI', 1956, 3, p. 106ff.
R.I. Curtis, *The Garum Shop of Pompeii (I, 12, 8),* in 'Cronache Pompeiane' V, 1979, p. 5ff.
J. Day, *Agriculture in the Life of Pompei*, in 'Yale Classical Studies' III, 1932, p. 165ff.
C. De Ruyt, *Macellum. Marché alimentaire des Romains*, Louvain, 1983.
R. Etienne, *La vita quotidiana a Pompei*, Milano, 1973.
ID., *A propos du vin pompéien*, in *Neue Forschungen in Pompeji*, Recklinghausen 1975, p. 309ff.
T. Frank, *The economic life of an ancient city*, in 'Classical Philology' XIII, 1918, p. 225ff.
E. Gabba, *Mercati e fiere nell'Italia romana*, in 'Studi Classici ed Orientali' 185, 1982, p. 141ff.
V. Gassner, *Die Kaufladen in Pompeji*, Wien 1986.
J. Heurgon, *Les Lassii Pompéiens et l'importation des vins italiens en Gaule*, in 'La Parola del Passato' 7, 1952, p. 113ff.
W.F. Jashemsky, *Giardini e vigneti in città*, in *Pompei 79,* cit., p. 119ff.
W.M. Jongman, *The economy and Society of Pompeii*, Amsterdam 1988.
J. Kolendo, *Le attività agricole degli abitanti di Pompei e gli attrezzi agricoli ritovati all'interno della città*, in 'Opus' 4, 1987, pp. 11-124.
G.F. La Torre, *Gli impianti commerciali ed artigianali nel tessuto urbano di Pompei*, in *Pompei. L'informatica al servizio di una città antica*, Roma, 1988, p. 75ff.
E. Lepore, *Orientamenti per la storia sociale di Pompei,* in 'Pompeiana', Napoli 1950, p. 144ff.
L'instrumentum domesticum di Ercolano e Pompei, Roma 1977.
O. Longo, P. Scarpi (ed.), *Nel nome del pane*, Bolzano 1996.
E. Magaldi, *Il commercio ambulante a Pompei*, in 'Atti Accademia Pontaniana' LX, 1930, p. 61ff.
B.J. Mayeske, *Bakeries, Baker and Bread at Pompeii*, Michigan 1972.
EAD., *A Pompeian Bakery on the Via dell'Abbondanza*, in *In Studia Pompeiana & Classica in honor of W.F. Jashemski*, 1, 1989, p. 149ff.
W. Moeller, *The Wool Trade of Ancient Pompeii*, Leiden, 1976.
D. Mustilli, *Botteghe di scultori, marmorarii, bronzieri e caelatores in Pompei*, in 'Pompeiana', Napoli 1950.
J. Packer, "*Inns at Pompeii*", in 'Cronache pompeiane' 4, 1978, pp. 5-53.
A. Tchernia, *Il vino: produzione e commercio*, in *Pompei 79*, Napoli, 1984, pp. 87-96.

Religious life

Alla scoperta di Iside, in 'La Parola del Passato' 49, 1994.
S. Adamo Muscettola, *Osservazioni sulla composizione dei larari con statuette in bronzo di Pompei ed Ercolano*, in *Toreutik und figürliche Bronzen römischer Zeit,* Akten der 6. Tagung über antike Bronzen 13-17 Mai 1980, Berlin 1984, pp. 9-32.
T.K. Boyce, *Corpus of the lararia of Pompeii*, in 'MemAmAc' 14, 1937
C. Cicirelli, *Vita religiosa nell'antica Pompei*, Napoli 1995.
R.M. Peterson, *The cults of Campania*, Roma 1919.
Pompei oltre la vita. Nuove testimonianze dalle necropoli, Napoli, 1998.
V. Tran Tam Tinh '*La vita religiosa*', in *Pompei 79*, cit., pp. 56-64.

Housing styles

J.P. Adam, *L'arte di costruire presso i Romani. Materiali e tecniche*, Milano 1984.
T. Budetta, M. Pagano, *Ercolano: legni e piccoli bronzi. Testimonianze dell'arredo e delle suppellettili della casa romana* (exhibition catalogue), Roma 1988.
R.C. Carrington, *Studies in the Campanian 'Villae Rusticae',* in 'Journal of Roman Studies' 21, 1931, pp. 110-130.
C. Chiaramonte Trerè, *Sull'origine e sviluppo dell'architettura residenziale di Pompei sannitica*, in 'ACME' 43,3, 1990, pp. 3-34.
J.R. Clarke, *The Houses of Roman Italy, 100 B.C. - A.D. 250. Ritual, Space, and Decoration,* Berkeley, 1991.
J.H. D'Arms, *Romans on the Bay of Naples: a social and cultural study of the villas and their owners from 150 B.C. to A.D. 400*, Cambridge, 1970.
ID, *Ville rustiche e ville di 'otium'*, in *Pompei 79*, cit., pp. 65-86.
E. De Albentiis, *La casa dei Romani*, Milano 1990.
F.J. Dwyer, *Pompeian Domestic Sculpture. A study of five Pompeian houses and their contents*, Roma 1982.
M. Della Corte, *Case ed abitanti di Pompei*, 3ed., Napoli, 1965.
L. Franchi Dell'Orto, A. Varone (eds.), *Riscoprire Pompei* (exhibition catalogue) Roma 1993.
E. Fabricotti, *I bagni nelle prime ville romane*, in 'Cronache Pompeiane' 2-3, 1976-77, pp. 29-111.

K. Gazda (ed.), *Roman Art in the private sphere. New Perspectives on the Architecture and Decor of the Domus, Villa, and Insula*, Ann Arbor 1991.
L. Grimal, *Les Jardins Romains à la fin de la république et aux deux premiers siècles de l'empire*, Paris, 1943.
M. Hoffmann, *L'architettura privata*, in *Pompei 79*, cit., p. 105ff.
W.F. Jashemski, *The Gardens of Pompeii, Herculanum and the Villas destroyed by Vesuvius*, I, New-York, 1979.
EAD., *The Gardens of Pompeii*, II, Appendices, New York, 1993.
A. Maiuri, *Portico e peristilio*, in 'La Parola del Passato' I, 1946, p. 306ff.
ID., *L'ultima fase edilizia di Pompei*, Roma 1942.
ID., *La casa a Pompei*, Napoli, 1951.
A. G. Mc Kay, *Houses, Villas and Palaces in the Roman World*, Itaka (1975) 1980.
H. Mielsch, *La villa romana*, Firenze, 1990.
F. Miele, *La casa a schiera I, 2,16, un esempio di edilizia privata a Pompei*, in 'Rivista di studi pompeiani' 3, p. 165ff.
C.F. Moss, *Roman Marble Tables*, Diss. Princeton, 1988.
F. e F. Niccolini, *Le case e i monumenti di Pompei disegnati e descritti*, Napoli 1854.
E. Pernice, *Die hellenistische Kunst in Pompeji VI. Pavimente und figürliche Mosaiken*, Berlin, 1938.
F. Pesando, *"Domus" Edilizia privata e società pompeiana fra III e I sec.a.C.*, (Monografie Sopr. Arch. di Pompei, 12), Roma, 1997.
Pompei. Abitare sotto il Vesuvio, Ferrara, 1996.
G.M.A. Richter, *The Furniture of the Greek, Etruscan and Romans*, London 1966.
A. Wallace-Hadrill, *Houses and Society in Pompeii and Herculaneum*, Princeton, 1994.
B. Zanker, *Pompei. Società, immagini urbane e forme dell'abitare*, Torino 1993.
F. Zevi (ed.), *Pompei*, I-II, Napoli, 1991-1992.

Wall and floor decorations

A. Barbet, *La peinture murale romaine. Les styles décoratifs pompéiens*, Paris 1985.
F.L. Bastet, M. de Vos, *Proposta per una classificazione del terzo stile pompeiano*, "Archeologische Studien van het Nederlands Instituut te Rom", 4, Den Haag, 1979.
H.G. Beyen, *Die pompejanische Wanddekoration vom zweiten bis vierten Stil*, I-II, Den Haag, 1938-1960.
R. Bianchi Bandinelli, *Tradizione ellenistica e gusto romano nella pittura pompeiana* (1941), in *Storicità dell'arte classica*, Roma, 1973, pp. 303-343.
M.E. Blake, *The Pavements of the Roman Buildings of the Republic and Early Empire*, in *MemAmAc* 8, Roma, 1930.
D. Corlaita Scagliarini, *Spazio e decorazione nella pittura pompeiana*, in 'Palladio' 23-25, 1974-76, pp. 3-44.
T. Fröhlich, *Lararien und Fassadenbilder in den Vesuvstädte. Untersüchungen zur volkstümlichen pompejanische Malerei*, Mainz, 1991.
W. Helbig, *Die Wandgemälde der vom Vesuv verschütteten Städte Campaniens*, 1868.
A. Laidlaw, *The First Style in Pompeii. Painting and Architecture*, Roma, 1985.
La pittura di Pompei. Testimonianze dell'arte romana nella zona sepolta dal Vesuvio nel 79 d.C., Milano, 1993.
A. Mau, *Geschichte der decorativen Wandmalerei in Pompeji*, Leipzig, 1882.
Pompeii. Picta fragmenta. Decorazioni parietali della città sepolta, Torino-Londra, 1997.
Pompei. Pitture e mosaici (Ist. Encicl. Ital. Treccani), vols. 1-9, Roma 1990-1997.
Romana Pictura. La pittura romana dalle origini all'età bizantina, Venezia 1998.
K. Schefold, *Vergessenes Pompeji*, Bern 1962.
ID., *La peinture pompéienne. Essai sur l'évolution de sa signification*, Coll. Latomus 108, Bruxelles, 1972.

Meals and banquets

A. Dosi, F. Schnell, *Le abitudini alimentari dei Romani* (Vita e costumi dei Romani antichi), 1, Roma 1992.
A. Dosi, F. Schnell, *I Romani in cucina* (Vita e costumi dei Romani Antichi), 3, Roma 1992.
E. Salza Prina Ricotti, *Ricette della cucina romana a Pompei e come eseguirle*, Roma 1993.

Walls and roads

Dove si cambia il cavallo (exhibition catalogue) 1995.
L. Garcia y Garcia, *Divisione fiorelliana e piano regolatore di Pompei*, in 'Opuscola Pompeiana' 3, Kyoto 1993, pp. 55-70.
A. Maiuri, *Studi e ricerche sulle fortificazioni di Pompei*, in 'Monumenti Antichi dell'Acc. dei Lincei' 33, 1929.
G.O. Onorato, *La sistemazione stradale del quartiere del Foro triangolare di Pompei*, in 'Rendiconti dei Lincei' 6, 1951, Fasc. 5-6, pp. 250-264.
G. Spano, *Porte e regioni pompeiane e vie campane*, in 'Rend. Acc. Lettere e Belle Arti di Napoli n. s. 17, 1937, pp. 267-360.
S. Tsujimura, *Ruts in Pompeii - The traffic system in the Roman city*, in 'Opuscola Pompeiana' 1, 1991, pp. 58-86.

Public and private lighting

Ercolano e Pompei. Sistemi di illuminazione nel primo secolo dopo Cristo (Pompeii exhibition 1994), Trecase, 1994.
G. Spano, *La illuminazione delle vie di Pompei*, in 'Rend.Acc.Nap.' n.s.7 (1919), 1920, pp. 1-128.

The water supply

E.B. Andersson, *Fountains and the Roman Dwelling - Casa del Torello in Pompeii*, in JdI 105, 1990.
ID. *Urban water supply in Pompeii and the sum of private water consumption*, in *La ciudad en el mundo romano* (Actas del XIV Congr. Intern. de arqueologia clasica, Tarragona 1993), vol. 2, Tarragona 1994, pp. 29-31.

I. Biera (ed.), *Utilitas necessaria-Sistemi idraulici nell'Italia Romana*, Milano 1994.

N. De Haan, G. C.M. Jansen (eds.), *Cura Aquarum in Campania*, Leiden 1996.

H. Eschebach, *Die Gebrauchswasserversorgung des antiken Pompeji*, in 'Antike Welt' 10,2, 1979, pp. 3-24.

E. Fassitelli, *Tubi e valvole dell'antica Roma*, Milano 1991.

A. Maiuri, *Pozzi e condutture d'acqua nell'antica città (Pompei)*, in 'Notizie degli Scavi', 1931, pp. 546-576.

N. Neuerburg, *L'architettura delle fontane e dei ninfei nell'Italia antica*, in 'Memorie Accademia Archeologia Lettere Belle Arti', 5, 1965.

M. Pagano, *L'apparato idrico dei giardini*, in *Domus-Viridaria-Horti Picti* (exhibition catalogue) Napoli 1992.

Latrines

R. Neudeker, *Die Pracht der Latrine. Zum Wandel öffentlicher Bedürfnisanstalten in der kaiserzeitlichen Stadt*, München 1994.

G. Jansen, *Water Systems and Sanitation in the Houses of Herculaneum*, in 'MededRom' 50, 1991, pp. 145-165.

EAD., *Paintings in Roman Toilets*, in *Functional and Spatial Analysis of Wall Painting* (Amsterdam 8-12 Sept. 1992), Leiden 1993, pp. 29-33.

Games and buildings for public performances

P. Ciancio Rossetto, G. Pisani Sartorio (eds.), *Teatri greci e romani. Alle origini del linguaggio rappresentato*, 3 vols., Roma, 1994-96.

F. Dupont, *Teatro e società a Roma*, Roma-Bari, 1991.

B. Gentili, *Lo spettacolo nel mondo antico*, Roma-Bari, 1977.

M. Gigante, 'La vita teatrale nell'antica Pompei', in *Studi salernitani in memoria di R. Cantarella*, Salerno, 1981.

J.C. Golvin, C. Landes, *Amphithéatres et gladiateurs*, Paris, 1990.

R. Graefe, *Vela erunt*, Mainz am Rhein, 1979.

P. Grimal, *Il teatro antico*, Napoli, 1994.

L. Jacobelli, *Gladiatori a Pompei*, Roma 2003

Q. Mancioli, *Giochi e spettacoli. Vita e costumi dei romani n. 4*, Roma, 1987.

R. Mitens, *Teatri greci e teatri ispirati all'architettura greca in Sicilia e nell'Italia meridionale c. 350-50 a.C.*, Roma 1988.

D. Nardoni, *i gladiatori romani*, Roma, 1989.

A. Neppi Modona, *Gli edifici teatrali greci e romani*, Firenze 1961.

R. Paris (ed.), *Persona. La maschera nel teatro antico*, Roma, 1990.

P. Sabbatini Tumolesi, *Gladiatorum Paria. Annunci di spettacoli gladiatori a Pompei*, Roma, 1980.

N. Savarese (ed.), *Teatri romani. Gli spettacoli nell'antica Roma*, Bologna 1996.

P. Veyne, *Il pane e il circo*, Bologna, 1984.

G. Ville, *La gladiature en Occident des origines à la mort de Domitien*, Roma, 1981.

H.W. Weber, *Panem et circenses. La politica dei divertimenti di massa nell'antica Roma*, Milano, 1989.

Thermal baths

Terme romane e vita quotidiana, Modena 1987.

P. Gallo, *Terme e bagni in Pompei antica*, Pompei, 1991.

L. Jacobelli, *Distribuzione degli impianti termali pubblici a Pompei: il caso delle Terme Suburbane*, in *La ciudad en el mundo romano. Actas del XIV Congr. Int. de arqueologia clasica (Tarragona 1993)*; vols. 2, Tarragona 1994, pp. 217-218.

Les thermes romains, Roma 1991.

H. Manderscheid, *Die Wasserbewirtschaftung Römischer Thermen. Archäologische und Hydrotechnische Untersuchungen*, Braunschweig, 1994.

I. Neilsen, *Thermae et Balnea. The Architecture and Cultural History of Roman Public Baths*, Aarhus 1990.

Inns and restaurants

M. Cretella, *Botteghe di Ercolano e Pompei*, Napoli, 1961.

E. Gibert, *Hôtelleries et hôteliers de Pompéi*, in 'Caesarodunum' 7 (1972), 1973, pp. 325-332.

T. Kleberg, *Hôtels, restaurants et cabaret dans l'antiquité romaine. Etudes historiques et philologiques*, Uppsala 1957.

Brothels and prostitution

N. Criniti (ed.), *Gli affanni del vivere e del morire*, Brescia 1991.

V. Vanoyeke, *La prostitution en Grèce et a Rome*, Paris 1990.

Bibliography of the individual monuments: apart from the well-known guides to Pompeii (in particular: A.M. De Vos, *Pompei, Ercolano, Stabia*, Roma-Bari 1982; E. La Rocca, M. e A. De Vos, F. Coarelli, *Guida archeologica di Pompei*, Milano 1976; P.G. Guzzo, A. D'Ambrosio, *Pompei*, Napoli 1998, new edition 2002)

The Temple of Venus

A. Mau, 'Tempel des Venus Pompeiana', in 'RomMitt.' XV, 1900, pp. 270-308.

L. Jacobelli, P. Pensabene, 'La decorazione architettonica del tempio di Venere a Pompei: contributo allo studio e alla ricostruzione del santuario' in 'Rivista Studi Pompeiani' VII (1995-96), 1998, pp. 45-75.

The Temple of Apollo

S. De Caro, *Saggi nell'area del Tempio di Apollo a Pompei*. In 'AION' 3, 1986.

The Basilica

A. Maiuri, *Saggi e ricerche intorno alla Basilica*, in 'Notizie Scavi' 1951, p. 225ff.

K. Ohr, *Die Basilika in Pompeji*, Berlin 1991.

The Forum and its monuments

A. Sogliano, *Il Foro di Pompei*, in 'Memorie Acc. Lincei', ser. VI, vol. I, 1925, p. 221ff.

K. Wallat, *Der Zustand des Forums von Pompeji am Vorabend des Vesuvausbruchs 79 n. Chr.*, in *Archäologie und Seismologie*, cit., pp. 75-92.

The Temple of Vespasian

G. Niebling, *Der Tempel und Altar des Vespasian in Pompeij*, in «Forschungen und Fortschrifte» 31, 1957, pp. 23-29.

The Forum baths

H. Eschebach, *La documentazione delle Terme del Foro a Pompei*, in *La regione sotterrata dal Vesuvio. Studi e prospettive*, Napoli 1982, p. 313ff.
A. Jorio, *Sistema di riscaldamento nelle antiche terme pompeiane*, in 'Boll. Comunale' 86, 1978-1979, pp. 167-189.

The House of the Faun

A. Hoffmann, *Ein rekonstruktionsproblem der Casa del Fauno in Pompeij*, 'Bericht Koldewey-Gesellschaft' 1978, pp. 35-41.
F. Pesando, *Auto celebrazione aristocratica e propaganda politica in ambiente privato: la casa del Fauno a Pompei*, in 'Cahiers du Centre G. Glotz' 7, 1996, pp. 189-228.
F. Zevi, *L'edilizia privata e la casa del Fauno*, in Pompei 1, Napoli 1991, pp. 47-74.
ID., *La casa del Fauno*, in *Pompei. Abitare sotto il Vesuvio* cit., pp. 37-47.

The House of the Vettii

A. Maiuri, *Pompei, casa dei Vetti*, in 'Bollettino d'Arte' 1927, p. 374ff.
W. Peters, *La composizione delle pareti dipinte nella Casa dei Vettii a Pompei*, in MEDED 39, 1977, pp. 95-128.
A, Sogliano, *La casa dei Vettii in Pompei*, in 'Monumenti Antichi Acc. Lincei' 8, 1898, pp. 3-97.

The Bakery (VII, 2, 22)

A. Mau, *Su certi apparecchi nei pistrini di Pompei*, 'RM'1, 1886, pp. 45-48.

The Triangular Forum and Doric Temple

J. A.K.E. de Waele, *The 'Doric' Temple on the Forum Triangulare in Pompeii*, in 'Opuscola Pompeiana 3, 1993, pp. 105-118.
L. Richardson Jr., *The Archaic Doric*

Temple of Pompeii, in 'La Parola del Passato' 29, 1974, pp. 281-290.

The Large Theatre

A. Maiuri, *Saggi nella cavea del Teatro Grande*, in 'Notizie degli Scavi' 1951, pp. 126-134.
G. Spano. *Il teatro delle Fontane in Pompei,* in 'MemNap'2 (1911), 1913, pp. 109-148.

The Small Theatre (Odeion)

O. T. Broneer, *The Odeum*, Cambridge, Mass. 1932.
M. Murolo, *Il cosidetto 'Odeo' in Pompei ed il problema della sua copertura*, in 'Rendiconti Acc. Di Arch. Lett. E Belle Arti di Napoli' n.s. 34, 1959, pp. 89-101.

The Temple of Isis

Alla ricerca di Iside. Analisi, studi e restauri dell'Iseo pompeiano nel Museo di Napoli, Roma 1992.
F.M. Avellino, *Il tempio di Iside a Pompei*, Napoli 1851.
O. Elia, *Le pitture del Tempio di Iside*, in 'Monumenti della Pittura Antica scoperti in Italia', Roma 1941.
Tran Tam Tinh, *Essai sur le culte d'Isis à Pompéi,* Paris 1964.

The Stabian Baths

H. Eschebach, *Die Stabianer Thermen in Pompeji*, Berlin 1979.

The Fullery of Stephanus

V. Spinazzola, *Pompei. Continuazione dello scavo della via dell'Abbondanza e scoperte quivi avvenute il mese di agosto 1912*, in 'Notizie degli Scavi' 1912, pp. 281-283.
ID., *Pompei alla luce degli Scavi Nuovi di Via dell'Abbondanza (anni 1910-1923)*, I-III, Roma 1953, pp. 763-785.
A. Uscatescu, *Fullonicae y tinctoriae en el mundo romano*, Barcelona, 1994.

The Thermopolium I, 8, 8

A. D'Ambrosio, *Il Termopolio e la casa di L. Vetuzio Placido,* in *Pompei. Abitare sotto il Vesuvio,* cit., pp. 109-113.

The House of Octavius Quartio or Loreius Tiburtinus

E. De Carolis, A. Ciarallo, E. Gallo,

La casa di D. Octavius Quartio (II, 2,2). Un esempio di giardino ricostruito sui dati di scavo, in *Parchi e giardini storici. Conoscenza, tutela e valorizzazione*, Roma 1991, pp. 170-171.
A. Maiuri, R. Pane, *La casa di Loreio Tiburtino e la Villa di Diomede in Pompei*, Roma 1947.

The Amphitheatre

M. Girosi, *L'Anfiteatro di Pompei*, in 'Memorie Acc. Arch. Lett e Belle Arti di Napoli' 5, 1936, pp. 29-55.

La Palestra

A. Maiuri, *Scavo della 'Grande Palestra' nel quartiere dell'Anfiteatro*, in 'Notizie degli Scavi' 1939, pp. 165-238.

The Necropolis of Porta Ercolano

V. Kockel, *Die Grabbauten vor dem Herkulaner Tor in Pompeji*, Mainz am Rhein, 1983.

The Villa of the Mysteries

A. Maiuri, *La Villa dei Misteri*, Roma 1931.

The graffiti and inscriptions of Pompeii are from the CIL (*Corpus Inscriptionum Latinarum*), published by the Academy of Berlin, vol. IV, edited by C. Zangemeister in 1871, by A. Mau in 1909 and by M. Della Corte and his successors R. Gruendel and F. Weber from 1952 to 1970. Inscriptions discovered subsequently are periodically catalogued in the *Année Epigraphique* (A.E), published in Paris.

Sources of illustrations

Illustrations are taken from the
followings works: Fausto and Felice
Niccolini, *Le Case ed i monumenti
di Pompei disegnati e descritti*, Napoli
1854-1896, Napoli, Soprintendenza
per i Beni Archeologici di Napoli
e Caserta (pp. 4-6, 15, 32, 48, 51-53,
55, 58, 61, 75, 108).
Plans in the section on *Monuments*
are from: A. Maiuri, R. Pane, *La
Casa di Loreio Tirburtino e la Villa
di Diomede in Pompei,* Roma 1947.
E. La Rocca, M. e A. De Vos, F.
Coarelli, *Guida Archeologica
di Pompei,* Verona 1976. *Pompei 79.
Raccolta di Studi per il decimonono
centenario dell'eruzione vesuviana,*
edited by F. Zevi, Napoli 1979.
I. Nielsen, *Thermae et Balnea,* Århus
1990. J.R. Clarke, *The Houses of
Roman Italy, 100 B.C. - A.D. 250.
Ritual, space and decoration,* Berkeley
1991. P. Zanker, *Pompei, Società,
immagini urbane e forme dell'abitare,*
Torino 1993. P.G. Guzzo,
A. d'Ambrosio, *Pompei. Guida
agli scavi,* Electa Napoli 1998,
new edition 2002.

Printed in June 2003
for Electa Napoli

Draft and final prints
SAMA, Quarto (Napoli)